The Quotable Eleanor Roosevelt

UNIVERSITY PRESS OF FLORIDA

Florida A&M University, Tallahassee
Florida Atlantic University, Boca Raton
Florida Gulf Coast University, Ft. Myers
Florida International University, Miami
Florida State University, Tallahassee
New College of Florida, Sarasota
University of Central Florida, Orlando
University of Florida, Gainesville
University of North Florida, Jacksonville
University of South Florida, Tampa
University of West Florida, Pensacola

The Quotable Eleanor Roosevelt

Edited by
Michele Wehrwein Albion

University Press of Florida

Gainesville/Tallahassee/Tampa/Boca Raton/Pensacola
Orlando/Miami/Jacksonville/Ft. Myers/Sarasota

Previous page: Eleanor Roosevelt with E. Gross (*left*) and P. C. Jessup at United Nations in Paris, September 22, 1948. Courtesy of the Franklin D. Roosevelt Library and Museum.

Copyright 2013 by Michele Wehrwein Albion

All rights reserved

Printed in the United States of America on acid-free paper

This book may be available in an electronic edition.

18 17 16 15 14 13   6 5 4 3 2 1

Library of Congress Cataloging-in-Publication Data
Albion, Michele Wehrwein.
The quotable Eleanor Roosevelt / edited by Michele Wehrwein Albion.
p. cm.
Includes bibliographical references.
ISBN 978-0-8130-4494-1 (alk. paper)
1. Roosevelt, Eleanor, 1884–1962—Quotations.
2. Presidents' spouses—United States—Quotations. I. Title.
E807.1.R48A25 2013
973.917092—dc23
2013015078

University Press of Florida
15 Northwest 15th Street
Gainesville, FL 32611-2079
http://www.upf.com

*For Zoe and Sarah, who,
like Eleanor Roosevelt,
are intelligent, articulate,
and not afraid to say what
they think*

Contents

Preface and Acknowledgments   ix

Chronology   xv

1 On Government and Politics   1

2 On Nations   21

3 On History, War, and Peace   31

4 On Religion   53

5 On Freedoms, Rights, and Threats to Them   61

6 On Work   67

7 On Money and Economics   75

8 On Arts, Literature, and Leisure   81

9 On Education and Learning   87

10 On Gender, Age, and Class   95

11 On Race and Ethnicity   111

12 On Humanity and Human Characteristics 125

13 On Emotions 141

14 On Relationships 149

15 Miscellaneous 161

16 On Herself 185

17 Eleanor Roosevelt on Others 199

18 Others on Eleanor Roosevelt 209

Notes 213

Bibliography 247

Preface and Acknowledgments

It has always seemed to me very unwise to quote people after they are dead. . . . They can no longer speak for themselves. They can neither explain why they did or said certain things, nor give the reasons which influenced them at the time. Therefore it seems to me that using past utterances to influence new decisions is not only unfair but very unwise.[1]

—Eleanor Roosevelt, October 25, 1945, "My Day"

Eleanor Roosevelt (ER)[2] is frequently quoted and often misquoted. Though she made this observation in reference to her husband, it may apply equally to her. The legendary First Lady's words are inscribed on everything from inspirational calendars to T-shirts and plaques, and are constantly posted on Twitter, Facebook, and other Internet sites. The statements are witty, smart, and moving, and often, they are wrongly attributed to ER.

One example is the statement: "Great minds discuss ideas, average minds discuss events, small minds discuss people." It sounds exactly like something ER would say. However, the first incarnation of the quote occurs in 1901 and is credited to Henry Thomas Buckle:

Men and women range themselves into three classes or orders of intelligence; you can tell the lowest class by their habit of always talking about persons; the next by the fact that their habit is always to converse about things; the highest by their preference for the discussion of ideas.[3]

By the late 1920s, the wording had been reduced to its current form. Frequently repeated during intervening years, misattribution to ER does not appear to have occurred until around the year 2000, when Internet usage became widespread. Though ER might wince at the prospect, this volume seeks to provide readers with a collection of definitive, documented statements made by Eleanor Roosevelt.

✵

ER was certainly a unique First Lady. Disinterested in perpetuating a White House culture of pleasant but empty social rituals, she was the first to hold her own press conferences, open only to female reporters. While previous first ladies refrained from public discussion of their personal views, ER granted interviews and wrote books, magazine articles, and a daily column espousing hers. Her frank conversations about political, social, and racial issues were an affront to many. She was seen as pushy and egotistical; clearly a woman who didn't know her place. But ER did know her place—beside her husband at a state dinner as well as deep within a mineshaft and blackened with coal dust.

In 1933, she entered an encampment of irate Bonus Marchers. The World War I veterans, impoverished by the Great Depression, were ready to riot. Within a few hours, she was leading the men in song. That same year, she flew with Amelia Earhart. She smiled bemusedly at those who called her an opportunist, a communist, or worse. During World War II, when the armed forces questioned the reliability of African American soldiers, she defied her Secret Service protectors and flew in an aircraft piloted by the Tuskegee Airmen. She later faced down the Ku Klux Klan with a bounty on her head. When asked what she would do if someone tried to assassinate FDR, she replied simply, "I'd step in front of him, of course."[4] She was brave. She was fearless. She was a woman ahead of her time.

❋

Source material for this book includes contemporary newspapers, interviews, letters, reminiscences of friends and relatives, her many published works, and radio and television interviews. Quotations attributed to Eleanor Roosevelt that could not be conclusively documented by a primary source or contemporary secondary source were omitted. The one exception is the quote, "Nobody can make you feel inferior without your consent." The earliest source for this statement is a tertiary source, *Reader's Digest*. Because the attribution, made twenty-two years before ER died, was widely distributed and was never contested by her, it has been included.

Judged by today's standards, ER's quotes often do not appear radical. It is important to keep in mind that in her day, most of the nation considered African Americans second-class citizens, and it was utterly unimaginable that one would someday be president. A woman's place was in the home, and those who wanted to work in business, industry, and academia were considered abnormal. Communism was not the passé bogeyman it is today, but a deadly threat to America; towns had fallout shelters, and children practiced duck-and-cover drills in preparation for a Russian nuclear attack that many feared was imminent.

Those who see ER's actions as foresighted or even revolutionary may be surprised by her use of language. She used tentative catchphrases like, "It seems to me," and "As I see it," which make her ensuing statements seem less emphatic. This was common for a generation of women who were seen as forward or presumptuous if they stated an opinion outright.

ER was generally careful about expressing her views. During World War II, she endorsed women serving in the armed forces but came short of calling for women in combat. As she would explain later in *This I Remember*, "I have grown more patient with age and have perhaps learned from my husband that no leader can be too far ahead of his followers."[5]

Many of ER's opinions changed over time. As a young woman, she held strong prejudices against Jews and other ethnic groups, but those opinions changed as she matured. In the case of communism, at first she preached education and tolerance. Later, as the Iron Curtain descended over Europe, she condemned the ideology, but never the people who lived under its rule.

While attempts have been made to capture the quotations verbatim, source material sometimes varies. Discrepancies are often attributed to the First Lady's speaking style. One reporter complained: "It was hard to take Mrs. Roosevelt's statements down. Her language was vague. You couldn't get it down fast. She kind of wandered. Covering her was the only time I wished I knew shorthand."[6]

When ER made several similar statements on the same topic with nuances of meaning, one has been selected. References to others are often listed in the endnotes.

Quotations are arranged by topic. Some dates are given as "circa" or, when there is no specific indication of the time period, they are left as "undated." Although ER died in 1962, some sources, like her book *Tomorrow Is Now*, were published posthumously and are arranged by the published date.

While the quotations seek to represent a broad spectrum of her life, there are some topics on which she seldom or never spoke. Though it irrevocably changed her relationship with her husband, she never publicly discussed FDR's affair with Lucy Mercer or how their marriage changed as a result of his infidelity. The subject of her own sexuality is not represented because there is insufficient documentation on the subject.

Additionally, though ER vigorously supported causes and organizations, some are underrepresented. For example, she wholeheartedly backed her husband's New Deal programs, but when discussing them, she kept on topic and seldom shared her own perspective and opinions. Similarly, though she highly valued her work at the United Nations, quotes on the subject are relatively limited.

Last, though the search for quotes has been exhaustive, it is by no means complete. In the future more source material may become available. Readers are invited to send additional quotations. Please include a source citation—even if it is incomplete—so that the quotations can be verified. Quotations may be sent to: Eleanor Roosevelt Quotations, P.O. Box 487, Dover, NH 03821, or to the comment section of the website: michelealbion.com.

✺

As a young person I frequently asked relatives who were old enough to have opinions of Eleanor Roosevelt what they thought of her. This was partly because I was intrigued by the warbling white-haired lady as a historic figure, but mostly because her mere name could elicit such different reactions. My great-grandfather, born in 1893, called her a "dangerous woman." The grandmother on the markedly less WASP side of my family admired her and thought it was about time that a woman was having her say.

After writing *The Quotable Edison* and *The Quotable Henry*

Ford, it was a thrill to research this admirable woman capable of such articulate and quotable quotes. There was so much remarkable material that editing the volume proved a great challenge.

☀

I am deeply grateful to a number of organizations and individuals who have helped to make *The Quotable Eleanor Roosevelt* possible. First and foremost is the Eleanor Roosevelt Papers Project. Begun in 2000, the Papers Project has amassed ER papers and publications and made them available to the public in book and digital form. These documents are not only available to scholars, but have been the basis of a public outreach effort by the Papers Project and George Washington University. In addition to cataloguing and making documents available, The Papers Project offers curricula and teaching aids, curates exhibits, offers programming on ER's human rights work, and mentors students.

Thank you also to Mark Renovitch and Robert Clark at the Franklin D. Roosevelt Presidential Library for their patience and assistance. Thanks to the kind folks at the Dover, New Hampshire, Public Library and the University of New Hampshire. Thanks to Marjorie Marcotte and Annelisa Wagner who assisted with editing, as well as my marvelous copy editor, Susan A. Murray. Three cheers to writing group, Writers on Words, for their constant encouragement. And, of course, thanks to my family: Matthew, Noah, Zoe, and Sarah, as well as my husband, Jim.

Chronology

October 11, 1884	Anna Eleanor Roosevelt (ER) born in New York City to Anna Hall and Elliott Roosevelt.
1891	Elliott, addicted to alcohol and narcotics, becomes violent and is committed to asylum.
	Brother, Hall Roosevelt, is born.
1892	Her mother dies. She and Hall move in with grandmother, Mary Ludlow Hall.
1894	Elliott dies of alcoholism.
1899–1902	Attends Allenswood School near London.
1903	Becomes engaged to Franklin D. Roosevelt (FDR) and volunteers at Rivington Street Settlement House.
March 17, 1905	Marries FDR. Lives in house adjoining mother-in-law, Sara Delano Roosevelt.
1906	Daughter Anna is born.
1907	Son James is born.
1909	Son Franklin D. Roosevelt Jr. is born and dies of influenza.
1910	Son Elliott is born.
	FDR is elected to state senate and family moves to Albany.
1912	Attends Democratic Party Convention.

1913	FDR appointed assistant secretary of the U.S. Navy and family moves to Washington, D.C.
1914	Gives birth to second son named Franklin Jr.
	FDR loses his primary bid for a U.S. Senate seat.
1916	Son John is born.
1918	Works for the Red Cross, U.S. Navy, and Navy League to assist World War I soldiers and attends the Paris Peace Conference.
1919	Works at the International Congress of Working Women, where she becomes friends with Rose Schneiderman and Maud Schwartz.
	Works with shell-shocked veterans at St. Elizabeth's Hospital.
1920	Campaigns for FDR for vice president.
	Joins League of Women Voters.
1921	FDR is struck by polio. Against her mother-in-law's wishes, ER encourages him to return to politics.
	Becomes friends with Elizabeth Read and Esther Lape.
1922	Joins the Women's Trade Union League and Women's Division of the Democratic State Committee, where she becomes friends with Marion Dickerman and Nancy Cook.
	Campaigns for Al Smith.
1923	Organizes and cochairs the Bok Peace Prize Committee with Esther Lape.
1924	Chairs women's platform committee at state Democratic convention
	Campaigns for gubernatorial candidate Al Smith and against her cousin, Republican Theodore Roosevelt Jr.
1925	Builds Val-Kill Cottage and establishes Val-Kill furniture factory at Hyde Park with Cook and Dickerman.

1926	Purchases the Todhunter School with Cook and Dickerman, where she teaches.
	Pickets with the Women's Trade Union League and is charged with disorderly conduct.
1927	Advocates for peace with Carrie Chapman Catt.
1928	With Al Smith, convinces FDR to run for governor.
1929	Becomes First Lady when FDR is elected governor.
	Refuses Secret Service protection, and Earl Miller becomes her bodyguard.
1930	Supports International Ladies' Garment Workers' Union strike.
1932	FDR is elected president.
	Begins friendship with reporter Lorena Hickok.
1933	Visits Bonus Army encampment in Virginia.
	Advocates for Arthurdale, West Virginia, coal-mine town.
	Holds first all-female press conferences.
	Writes *It's Up to the Women*.
1934	Joins National Association for the Advancement of Colored People and National Urban League. Lobbies for old-age pensions and antilynching legislation.
1935	Visit to Ohio coal mine sparks heated debate on the role of the First Lady.
	Begins publishing "My Day" column.
1936	FDR is reelected.
1937	Cancels a Lancaster, Pennsylvania, speech when she learns the club excludes Jews.
	Writes *This Is My Story*.
1938	Writes *This Troubled World*.

1939	Resigns from the Daughters of the American Revolution over exclusion of the African American singer Marian Anderson from Constitution Hall.
1940	Speaks at the Democratic National Convention.
	Writes *The Moral Basis of Democracy.*
1941	Begins "If You Ask Me" question-and-answer column.
1942	Flies with the Tuskegee Airmen.
	Travels to Britain to support British and Allied forces.
1943	Tours South Pacific to support American and Allied troops.
1944	Travels through Caribbean and South America touring hospitals and military bases.
1945	FDR dies.
1946	Refuses a congressional pension.
	Elected head of the United Nations Human Rights Commission and begins to draft Declaration of Human Rights.
	Visits Zeilsheim displaced-persons camp in Germany.
1947	Supports a separate Jewish state.
1948	Threatens to resign from United Nations if Truman fails to recognize the State of Israel.
1949	Criticized by Cardinal Spellman for opposition to federal aid for parochial schools.
	Writes *This I Remember.*
1952	Campaigns for Adlai Stevenson.
	Travels to Lebanon, Syria, Israel, Jordan, Pakistan, India, Nepal, Burma, Indonesia, Thailand, Singapore, the Philippines, and Chile.
	Resigns from United Nations after election of Eisenhower.

1953	Opposes House Un-American Activities Committee hearings.
	Travels to Japan, Hong Kong, Turkey, Greece, and Yugoslavia
	Writes *India and the Awakening East* and *UN Today and Tomorrow.*
1954	Writes *Ladies of Courage* with Hickok and *It Seems to Me.*
1955	Supports Montgomery bus boycott.
	Travels to Israel, Japan, Hong Kong, Indonesia, Cambodia, and the Philippines.
1956	Campaigns for Adlai Stevenson.
1957	Visits the Soviet Union and Morocco.
	The Ku Klux Klan offers $25,000 to kidnap her.
1958	Speaks at Highlander Folk School despite Ku Klux Klan threats.
	Visits the Soviet Union.
	Writes *On My Own.*
1959	Testifies to Congress in support of the minimum wage.
	Travels to Israel and Iran.
1960	Campaigns for John F. Kennedy.
	Writes *You Learn by Living.*
1961	Writes *The Autobiography of Eleanor Roosevelt.*
	Appointed to United Nation and as chair of President's Commission on the Status of Women.
1962	Tours Israel.
	Writes *Eleanor Roosevelt's Book of Common Sense Etiquette* and *Tomorrow Is Now*
	Dies from tuberculosis on November 7, at the age of seventy-eight.

Franklin and Eleanor Roosevelt on Inauguration Day, 1941. Courtesy of the Franklin D. Roosevelt Library and Museum.

1 ✸ On Government and Politics

Though her uncle Theodore was elected president when she was fifteen, Eleanor Roosevelt showed little interest in government and political affairs until she attended Allenswood, a French-language boarding school in London. There, immersed in the study of history and contemporary politics, ER developed her own opinions and defended them in vigorous school debates.

ER set aside many of her personal interests, including politics, when she married FDR in 1905. The needs and interests of others continued to come first as she raised their children. During World War I, her horizons broadened as she devoted herself to the war effort. Later, after FDR contracted polio, ER was asked to keep the Roosevelt name alive in New York State politics. She succeeded, becoming a well-regarded Democratic Party leader.

In 1924, ER actively campaigned against her cousin, Theodore Roosevelt Jr., in favor of New York Governor Al Smith. Smith lost the 1928 bid for president, but FDR was elected to his previous office, New York governor, and ER became First Lady of the state.

ER was not interested in the largely ceremonial role of a traditional First Lady, so she and FDR made a deal. She would function as the governor's wife and pursue her own interests, speaking, writing, and teaching at the Todhunter School.[1] In addition, though neither publicly admitted it, ER advised FDR on policies and made suggestions for appointments.[2]

ER hoped for a similar compromise when FDR became president, but the White House was not the governor's mansion. When she expressed her opinions, she was mocked as "Madam President" and "Empress Eleanor," and accused of attempting to influence policy.[3] She was vilified for her journalistic work as well as for hosting conferences solely for female members of the press. But no one complained when, shortly after her husband took office, ER defused escalating tensions with World War I Bonus Marchers, prompting the phrase, "Hoover sent the army, Roosevelt sent his wife."[4]

ER firmly believed the government should play an active role in the lives of Americans. When the Great Depression crippled the nation, she supported her husband's New Deal relief programs, but not unequivocally. She criticized the Federal Emergency Relief Administration and the Civil Works Administration for excluding women and blacks.

One of her best-known efforts was Arthurdale, a West Virginia New Deal community populated by white coal miners, subsistence farmers, and their families. She secured government services and private donations, lifting the residents out of abject poverty. Unfortunately, improved conditions came with a staggering $2 million price tag.[5]

ER always believed in the power of democracy, but her opinion of communism changed over time. During the 1930s, she encouraged tolerance, despite her personal opposition to the ideology. After World War II, however, as the Iron Curtain descended over Eastern Europe, she increasingly spoke out against Soviet aggression and oppression. Her opposition to communism became more intense after she visited the Soviet Union in 1957 and 1958.

Following FDR's death, journalists and politicians assumed ER would run for office. She refused and planned for a quiet retirement. Instead, she was soon speaking at political conventions, campaigning for local, state, and national Democratic candidates, and quietly advising President Truman.

Of all of her accomplishments, ER was proudest of her role in the United Nations. Appointed as a delegate by President Truman in 1946, she chaired the Commission on Human Rights, which was charged with drafting the Universal Declaration of Human Rights. ER and her committee finessed opposing sides, and the Declaration was unanimously passed on December 10, 1948.[6]

On Government

The very weaknesses of human nature are what make it so important that we keep a constantly watchful eye on our government, and that in turn our government watches us with equal care.[7]

October 23, 1942, "My Day"

The Government reflects the attitude of the people . . . the fault of bad things in our country lies with the average citizen who will take no interest in the country's affairs.[8]

October 21, 1943, *Western Mail* (Perth, Australia)

Research and training are two things which are essential to the health of the nation. They should not depend upon private funds alone.[9]

September 7, 1945, "My Day"

Indifference, apathy, unwillingness on the part of good people to go down into the arena and fight, will give any city or any country poor government.[10]

November 8, 1945, "My Day"

On Politics

I feel rather sad about politics. There are so many out there who are for themselves and not for the good of the country in both parties.[11]

January 10, 1920, letter to Isabella Ferguson

America must come first, not party.[12]

Circa September 1921

Bad methods of government, graft and poor public servants arise largely from the individual citizen's lack of interest in politics.[13]

August 9, 1938, "My Day"

I hate to see us put so much trust in polls. After all, they don't represent reasoned thought.[14]

January 17, 1939, White House press conference

Sometimes I wonder if we shall ever grow up in our politics and say definite things which mean something, or whether we shall always go on using generalities to which everyone can subscribe, and which mean very little.[15]

July 1, 1940, "My Day"

Any group would profit by the study of history and would learn what brings about poor administration—the hates and jealousies among people who should be interested primarily in the achievement of certain results, but who rarely can separate their objectives from their own personal ambitions.[16]

June 13, 1944, "My Day"

[I]n political life I have never felt that anything really mattered but the satisfaction of knowing that you stood for the things in which you believed, and had done the very best you could.[17]

November 8, 1944, "My Day"

The obstructionist methods of the filibuster seem to me to make no sense. They destroy democratic government and leave the people in the position where their representatives waste hours and days of precious time, not gaining any new information, but simply being worn out. . . . This seems to me a negation of real democracy.[18]

July 2, 1945, "My Day"

I have long felt that the same amount [of money] should be spent by both parties, that both should be given free radio and television time, and that an equal amount of newspaper advertising and railroad travel time should be allowed in different categories and paid for by the public.[19]

February 13, 1957, "My Day"

Politics is the participation of the citizen in his government. The kind of government he has depends entirely on the quality of that participation.[20]

Circa 1960, *You Learn by Living*

On Politicians

Politician: A public servant unselfishly giving his time to carry out the wishes of a majority of the people and devoting to that task all his education and experience.[21]

May 1, 1935, on her own definition of a politician

A man who chooses to hold public office must learn to accept the slander as part of the job and to trust that the majority of people will judge him by his accomplishments in public service.[22]

Circa 1949, *This I Remember*

An important ingredient for the politician is the ability to attract and draw people to him. All political action is filtered through other human beings.[23]

Circa 1960, *You Learn by Living*

A good public servant becomes so at a high cost of personal sacrifice. We need such men; when we find them we owe them our gratitude and, above all, our respect.[24]

Circa 1960, *You Learn by Living*

Our trouble is that we do not demand enough of the people who represent us. . . . [W]e must spur them to more imagination and enterprise in making a push into the unknown; we must make clear that we intend to have responsible and courageous leadership.[25]

Circa 1963, *Tomorrow Is Now*

On Political Conventions

I listened [to the convention] last night & wondered if in 1783 they whooped it up so much. It seems undignified & meaningless but perhaps we need it![26]

June 27, 1936, letter to Lorena Hickok, on the Democratic Convention of 1936

The circus has almost overshadowed the serious purpose and far-reaching effect of these deliberations.[27]

Circa 1961, *The Autobiography of Eleanor Roosevelt*, on the Democratic Convention of 1960

[I]t would appear that the same tactics are used in both parties. In both cases, one had the feeling that the convention did not greatly matter. The votes had been sewed up beforehand.[28]

Circa 1961, *The Autobiography of Eleanor Roosevelt*

On Political Parties

Sometimes I wonder if it will take the suffering of the peoples in conquered countries and those who are still fighting for their freedom today, to make us realize that there are times when it matters little whether you are a Republican or a Democrat.[29]

January 7, 1941, "My Day"

No party would probably meet one's desires all the time & yet organization is the only way to have strength & some party discipline is essential.[30]

July 3, 1944, letter to Joseph P. Lash

I am not beholden to my Party. What I give, I give freely and I am too old to want to be curtailed in any way in the expression of my own thinking.[31]

July 9, 1946, *Look*

[It is] cowardly to go over to the other party. One should fight to make the party that represents—or should represent—the ideals one believes in as good as it ought to be.[32]

October 4, 1959, *New York Times*

The morality of a party must grow out of the conscience and the participation of the voters.[33]

Circa 1961, *The Autobiography of Eleanor Roosevelt*

On Democrats and Republicans

I feel strongly that the Democrats should remain in power if we can free ourselves to the extent of at least controlling our reactionary Southerners.[34]

May 26, 1945, letter to Secretary of the Interior Harold Ickes

I believe that the Democratic Party, at least the progressive part of the Democratic Party, represents the only safe way we have of moving forward in this country. I believe that the liberal-minded Democrats hold to the only international policy which can bring us a peaceful world.[35]

July 9, 1946, *Look*

[T]he Democratic Party has been in the past more interested in measures which would be a help to the average citizen. The Democratic Party has been more ready to try new things, to meet new situations, and has been more alert to the dangers as they loomed on the horizon in international situations.[36]

Circa 1946, *If You Ask Me*

I hope so.[37]

Circa 1946, *If You Ask Me*, on if she had any good friends who were Republicans

I know we need a united party. But it cannot be a united party that gives up its principles. . . . I welcome every kind of liberal.[38]

December 21, 1959, *Life,* response to Harry Truman's criticism of members of his own party

On the Presidency and Her Husband's Presidency

Gee! I wish I could be excited about all this, I can't & I hate myself![39]

June 27, 1936, letter to Lorena Hickok, on her husband's 1936 run for president

If F.D.R. wins I'll be glad for him & for the country & if he loses I'll be glad for myself & the kids![40]

October 22, 1940, letter to Lorena Hickok, on her husband's 1940 run for president

What a weight of responsibility this one man at the desk, facing the rest of the people, has to carry. Not just for this hemisphere alone, but for the world as a whole![41]

May 29, 1941, "My Day"

Is there anything we can do for you? For you are the one in trouble now.[42]

April 12, 1945, response to Harry Truman, who, following the death of FDR, asked what he could do for her

Franklin's death ended a period in history and now in its wake those of us who laid in his shadow have to start again under our own momentum and wonder what we can achieve.[43]

April 19, 1945, letter to Lorena Hickok

You will have pressures from every side. I am sure your own wisdom and experience and faith in God will guide you aright.[44]

August 15, 1945, letter to President Truman

Any President frequently suffers from his friends as much as from his enemies, and it is in the sense of loyalty and gratitude which often gets men in public life into the greatest of trouble.[45]

March 1, 1946, letter to President Truman

On Democracy

A democratic form of government is dependent for its success on an informed voter. It is only easy to over throw democracy where the sources of information are not available to the average citizen.[46]

August 21, 1936, "My Day"

I believe that democracy is based on the ability to make democracy serve the good of the majority of the people. If it can't do that, then it should not live.[47]

June 17, 1937, *New York Times*

We need not fear any isms if our democracy is achieving the ends for which it was established.[48]

Circa 1938, response to concerns about socialism and communism

The success or failure of democracy boils itself down to two things, freedom and security. Freedom boils down to a chance to work and earn a living at your work.[49]

May 22, 1939, White House press conference

It is an indisputable fact that democracy cannot survive where force and not law is the ultimate court of appeal.[50]

January 1939, *Virginia Quarterly Review*

Under a dictatorship it may be sufficient to learn to read and write and to do certain things by rote, but in a democracy we must learn to reason and to think for ourselves.[51]

June 15, 1940, *Collier's*

The citizens of Democracy must model themselves on the best and most unselfish life we have known in history. They may not all believe in Christ's divinity, though many will; but His life is important simply because it becomes a shining beacon of what success means. If we once establish this human standard as a measure of success, the future of Democracy is secure.[52]

Circa 1940, "The Moral Basis of Democracy"

Perhaps the greatest sacrifice of all is the necessity which Democracy imposes on every individual to make himself decide in what he believes.[53]

Circa 1940, "The Moral Basis of Democracy"

[I]t seems to me that Democracy has one great advantage over Communism—it really requires the participation of every citizen in the choice of the people to fill government office.[54]

September 30, 1941, "My Day"

A democracy can never succeed unless each individual takes responsibility for his nation, its policies and the representatives he elects.[55]

May 26, 1943, "My Day"

In democratic countries the people must think for themselves.[56]

September 6, 1943, *Argus* (Melbourne, Australia)

We are only just beginning to realize that the obligations of democracy outweigh the privileges.[57]

October 21, 1943, *Western Mail* (Perth, Australia)

Somehow we must be able to show people that democracy is not about words, but action.[58]

Circa 1953, *India and the Awakening East*

We must, of course, tell the truth and acknowledge our failures, but we should constantly cite examples showing that we are continually planning and striving for a more perfect democracy.[59]

Circa 1953, *India and the Awakening East*

[W]e stand before the world on trial, really, to show what democracy means, and that is a heavy responsibility, because the world today is deciding between democracy and Communism, and one means freedom and the other means slavery.[60]

August 13, 1956, letter to Harry Truman

To me, the democratic system represents man's best and brightest hope of self-fulfillment, of a life rich in promise and free from fear; the one hope, perhaps, for the complete development of the whole man. But I know, and learn more clearly every day, that we cannot keep our system strong and free by neglect, by taking it for granted, by giving it our second-best attention.[61]

Circa 1961, *The Autobiography of Eleanor Roosevelt*

It seems to me that America's objective today should be to try to make herself the best possible mirror of democracy that she can.[62]

Circa 1961, *The Autobiography of Eleanor Roosevelt*

A respect for the rights of other people to determine their forms of government and their economy will not weaken our democracy. It will inevitably strengthen it. One of the first things we must get rid of is the idea that democracy is tantamount to capitalism.[63]

Circa 1963, *Tomorrow Is Now*

In the final analysis, a democratic government represents the sum total of the courage and the integrity of its individuals. It cannot be better than they are.[64]

Circa 1963, *Tomorrow Is Now*

Democracy requires both discipline and hard work. It is not easy for individuals to govern themselves. . . . It is one thing to gain freedom, but no one can give you the right to self-government. This you must earn for yourself by long discipline.[65]

Circa 1963, *Tomorrow Is Now*

On Socialism and Communism

If we are not going to find remedies in Progressivism then I feel sure the next step will be Socialism.[66]

Circa 1912, letter to her aunt Maude Waterbury, expressing concern that poverty might drive Americans to socialism

I am sure the more you study communism or socialism, the more tolerant you will feel. The very best thing would be to travel to such countries and see for yourself. We are not afraid of a known situation. It's the unknown that we fear.[67]

Circa 1930–39

I am now and always will be opposed to the Communist form of government.[68]

January 25, 1940, "My Day"

I am not afraid of the Communists in the United States. They are a very small group, and my feeling has always been that as long as the needs of our people are met by our own form of government, democracy need have no fear of the growth of other ideas, either in the field of economics or of government.[69]

June 9, 1945, "My Day"

The economy of communism is an economy which grows in an atmosphere of misery and want.[70]

February 12, 1947, "My Day"

[I]t always used to rather amuse me to be labeled as a Communist because I couldn't resist what the Communists might think of having me wished on them. . . . [N]ow that the Russians know me a little better they are apparently quite sure, not only that I am NOT a Communist, but that they don't want me.[71]

November 17, 1948, radio broadcast

What I really consider the greatest danger in Communism is its creation of a police state, which puts everybody under such terror that there is no free expression of individual thinking and no dignity for the human being. The evil of Communism as it has developed in Europe is, of course, the same evil which existed in Fascism and Nazism.[72]

September 1953, *McCall's Magazine*

On Despotism

[F]or all despotism is based on education which holds people to a definite pattern and crushes individually.[73]

March 21, 1936, "My Day"

It is undeniably true that a benevolent despot can quickly bring about better conditions and avoid suffering for the people as a whole, but one cannot always count on a despot being benevolent![74]

February 1950, *McCall's Magazine*

On Patriotism

[I]t is sometimes difficult to decide where common sense and patriotism end and self-interest begins.[75]

March 23, 1942, "My Day"

Outward behavior, while important, is not the real measure of a man's patriotism.[76]

Circa 1962, *Eleanor Roosevelt's Book of Common Sense Etiquette*

True patriotism springs from a belief in the dignity of the individual, freedom and equality not only for Americans but for all people on earth, universal brotherhood and good will, and a constant striving toward the principles and ideals on which this country was founded.[77]

Circa 1962, *Eleanor Roosevelt's Book of Common Sense Etiquette*

On Citizenship

I feel that any citizen should be willing to give all that he has to give to his country in work or sacrifice in times of crisis.[78]

January 21, 1941, "My Day"

We must all of us come to look upon our citizenship as a trusteeship, something that we exercise in the interest of the whole people.[79]

February 6, 1941, *New York Times*

If we are going to take our citizenship seriously, every man, woman and child will have an obligation to his community—and the first one which we should face today and begin to plan for, is the obligation towards children.[80]

July 11, 1942, "My Day"

We know that this citizenship requires a constant discipline of ourselves, an examination of our every action and of our every thought to make sure of its honesty of purpose. We know that it means we cannot be mean, small or selfish, because on us depends the attitude of our nation, and our nation has the potentialities of greatness and power.[81]

August 24, 1943, "My Day"

As individuals we feel sometimes we can do very little, but in a democracy, each individual has to fully live up to the obligations of his citizenship. Unless he expresses himself, those obligations may go unfulfilled. So each of us has the obligation to know how to make our citizenship count.[82]

June 22, 1944, "My Day"

The riches of a nation are its people, but they must have a vision of what they can accomplish, or they will fall short of their desired achievement.[83]

July 22, 1944, "My Day"

I do believe that every citizen, as long as he is alive and able to work, has an obligation to work on public questions and that he should choose the kind of work he is best fitted to do.[84]

July 9, 1946, *Look*

The chief duty of the citizen is to make his government the best possible medium for the peaceful and prosperous conduct of life.[85]

Circa 1960, *You Learn by Living*

If they have no capacity for development, and no enterprise beyond sitting glued to a television screen, they will deteriorate as human beings, and we will have a great mass of citizens who are of no value to themselves or to their country or to the world.[86]

Circa 1961, *The Autobiography of Eleanor Roosevelt*

Our impact on the rest of the world is the sum total of what each of us does as a private citizen.[87]

Circa 1963, *Tomorrow Is Now*

On Voting

If young men of eighteen and nineteen are old enough to be trained to fight their country's battles and to proceed from training to the battlefields, I think we must accept the fact that they are also old enough to know why we fight this war.[88]

January 21, 1943, "My Day," support for dropping the national voting age from twenty-one to eighteen

I would think it fairly obvious that any citizen in a democracy would want to use his vote.[89]

December 3, 1943, "My Day"

We must be concerned, and we must all use our precious right to vote and use it wisely. If we do, we just may be able to lead the way to a more peaceful and democratic world.[90]

Circa 1947

On Taxes

We may pay high taxes, but if it means that many hard working people have better lives, then I am glad to do so.[91]

May 31, 1937, "My Day"

Several people have asked me to explain why I am opposed to the sales tax. The reason is that I believe an income tax will bring in more revenue and will be, on the whole, a more clear-cut and far-reaching way of making us all realize the need for a contribution. It will not affect the lowest income group, which can barely meet the daily necessities of living.[92]

November 3, 1943, "My Day"

It is a sugarcoated tax and you do not always realize why a given thing you buy is costing more.[93]

November 3, 1943, "My Day," on sales taxes

On Social Security

I think, pretty well throughout the country, that it is the right of old people when they have worked hard all their lives, and, through no fault of theirs, have not been able to provide for their old age, to be cared for in the last years of their life.[94]

February 1934, speech entitled "Old Age Pensions," given to the D.C. Branch of the American Association for Social Security

On Foreign Policy

It behooves us to look for ways in which we can make friends with the other nations, for the results of future wars, if we do not prevent them, will be disastrous to all of us.[95]

March 2, 1943, "My Day"

Yet the art of diplomacy was meant to teach us to do what has to be done truthfully, in straightforward fashion, but with courtesy and consideration for those with whom we deal. This requires a certain amount of imagination and the ability to put oneself in the other fellow's place—something which of late we have not always found it easy to do.[96]

August 24, 1945, "My Day"

Failures in understanding among nations and in goodwill cannot be accepted in the future. They are tantamount to self-destruction.[97]

October 6, 1945, "My Day"

I do not believe the Russians want to go to war. Neither do we[,] but I think the ingenuity to find ways to get what we want rests with us.[98]

June 7, 1947, letter to President Truman

We are in a world where force still is the ultimate way of deciding questions. It should be law, but it still isn't law; it still is force.[99]

June 1948, *Christian Register*

We owe it to ourselves and to the world, to our own dignity and self-respect, to set our own standards of behavior, regardless of what other nations do.[100]

April 1961, *Atlantic Monthly*

Our obligation to the world is, primarily, an obligation to our own future.[101]

Circa 1961, *The Autobiography of Eleanor Roosevelt*

In dealing with the new nations of the world, we must learn the meaning of that noble word *respect*. That is the only sound and enduring basis for any relationship among peoples, as it is among individuals. We must learn to respect the various methods of development of the new nations, so long as they grant the individuals certain basic rights. We cannot say to them, "If you will accept our way of life we will help you." If we are going to build a strong and peaceful world, we must be intelligent enough to help new nations in terms of their needs and not of our personal theories.[102]

Circa 1963, *Tomorrow Is Now*

On the United Nations

I can quite understand why men like Prof. [Albert] Einstein feel that a world government would answer the problem.... If nations find it so hard to agree on the minor points at issue today, how do any of these hopeful people think that a world government could be made to work?[103]

January 29, 1948, "My Day." Following the bombings of Hiroshima and Nagasaki, Einstein believed a world government was the only hope of preventing the use and spread of nuclear weapons.

We should remember that the United Nations is not a cure-all. It is only an instrument capable of effective action when its members have a will to make it work.[104]

July 22, 1952, speech to the Democratic National Convention

We must keep the faith, strive to strengthen the U.N. which is the one machine through which we must work for greater understanding and eventually, we hope, for a peaceful world.[105]

July 23, 1952, *Wallingford (Conn.) Meriden Daily Journal*

[I] have come to feel with ever-increasing conviction that work with and through the United Nations is the keystone to success in developing co-operation among countries and to peace in the future.[106]

Circa 1953, *India and the Awakening East*

After all, it is because it is an effective organization that Mr. Khrushchev has been so determined to destroy it.[107]

Circa 1961, *The Autobiography of Eleanor Roosevelt.* Nikita Khrushchev famously banged his shoe on his desk at the U.N. to protest a delegate's comments about Soviet expansion.

Eleanor Roosevelt being greeted in Japan, May 1953. Courtesy of the Franklin D. Roosevelt Library and Museum.

2 ✳ On Nations

Eleanor Roosevelt's comments about other nations and ethnic groups were mostly private musings made to close friends and relatives. Some represent keen observations, while others expose prejudices. Many quotes reflect her reaction to the historical or political climate of her times.

As she matured, ER became more accepting of individuals from a variety of cultures and nationalities. Part of this growth was influenced by travel. She attended boarding school in Europe and returned during World War I when her husband was secretary of the U.S. Navy. During the Second World War, she traveled alone, first to England, then through the South Pacific. After FDR's death, she continued to travel. In 1952 alone, she visited Lebanon, Israel, Trans-Jordan, Syria, Pakistan, India, Nepal, Burma, Indonesia, Singapore, and the Philippines. In 1953, she visited Japan and in 1957, the Soviet Union.[1]

ER took great pride in being an American. She admired the nation's democratic beliefs, work ethic, and can-do spirit. This pride was tempered by her assertion that the privileges of citizenship came with the responsibility of being an informed, active, and responsible citizen.

On the British and Great Britain

There is no use thinking that because the British speak English we shall automatically be friends. We sometimes find their particular brand of English hard to understand and they look upon ours as equally odd.[2]

June 30, 1942, "My Day"

Great Britain is always anxious to have some one pull her chestnuts out of the fire, and though I am very fond of the British individually and like a great many of them, I object very much to being used by them.[3]

November 20, 1945, letter to Harry Truman

[S]ome English people, particularly the traveling English, have a genius for doing and saying the wrong thing.[4]

Circa 1946, *If You Ask Me*

On China

China has never been a united nation. The Chinese people have still to learn how to live with one another as a unified people.[5]

December 5, 1945, *Boston Post*

On the French and France

[N]othing can down the Parisian woman's chic.[6]

September 2, 1944, "My Day," comment on Parisians' ability to remain fashionable despite wartime deprivations

The people take longer to enjoy life as they live it here, and I am not sure they may not get more of it than we do at home.[7]

December 3, 1948, "My Day," on her visit to Paris

[T]he thing we call French culture may be due to the fact that French children can play, surrounded by the things of the past, palaces of bygone kings, statues, remembrances of history.[8]

Circa 1960, *You Learn by Living*

On Germans and Germany

All of us who know Germans are aware that they like to be governed, but this attitude should not be encouraged. They should be made to realize that they are responsible for their leaders and their form of government.[9]

September 29, 1945, letter to Ben L. Rose

Not the Russians, but the Germans have brought about the past two world wars.[10]

October 13, 1945, "My Day"

On Indians and India

The new Constitution abolishes Untouchability and guarantees all people equal rights before the law. But, as we know in our own country, it is one thing to abolish discrimination in the Constitution and another to put it into nation-wide practice.[11]

Circa 1953, *India and the Awakening East*

As long as I live I shall carry in my mind the beauty of the Taj, and at last I know why my father felt it was the one unforgettable thing he had seen in India. He always said it was the one thing he wanted us to see together.[12]

Circa 1953, *India and the Awakening East*

On Israel

I do not happen to be a Zionist.[13]

November 20, 1945, letter to President Truman

For my part I would like to see Palestine opened to the homeless Jews of the world.[14]

December 15, 1946, *New York Times Magazine*

What astounds one in Israel is that the spirit is like the American spirit. There is imagination to accomplish great projects and no fear of undertaking them.[15]

February 20, 1952, "My Day"

I hope that all of us in the United States recognize the fact that Israel is the one state in the whole Near East that understands the meaning of freedom and democracy.[16]

April 30, 1958, "My Day"

On Norwegians and Norway

The Norwegians don't give me much excitement but they are nice to look at![17]

July 1, 1943, letter to Trude W. Pratt

On Russia, Russians, and the Soviet Union (see also "On Communism")

She [Russia] is an unknown quantity. Her strength is not yet measured. The fact that she has done in some 25 years what the rest of Europe has taken several hundred years to do gives many a sense of insecurity.[18]

June 1, 1945, "My Day"

I don't see why we can't start thinking of the Russians as individual people rather than as we get a picture of them as a great big bear.[19]

January 5, 1945, press conference

They do have an inferiority complex, but they also have tenacity. We shall have to work very hard to understand them, because they start from a different background.[20]

February 16, 1946, *New York Times*

The Russians, like the [Ku Klux] Klan, apparently do not believe in equal rights, although they—like the Klan—would not admit this.[21]

December 22, 1948, radio broadcast

The Soviet children have little or no desire for freedom. Their conditioning and training has been carefully thought out to prevent deviation of any kind, on any level, from birth to death.[22]

Circa 1961, *The Autobiography of Eleanor Roosevelt*

There is no fear of eggheads in Russia.[23]

Circa 1961, *The Autobiography of Eleanor Roosevelt*, reaction to Soviet respect for intelligence and education

They have no freedom, we say. But they never had freedom, so they do not miss it.[24]

Circa 1961, *The Autobiography of Eleanor Roosevelt*

On Americans and the United States

We can only have a unified country if we have the feeling that everybody is working for the good of everybody else.[25]

June 28, 1940, *New York Times*

America is not a pile of goods, more luxury, more comforts, a better telephone system, a greater number of cars. America is a dream of greater justice and opportunity for the average man and, if we can not obtain it, all our other achievements amount to nothing.[26]

January 6, 1941, "My Day"

Only with equal justice, equal opportunity, and equal participation in the government can we expect to be a united country.[27]

March 1941, *Common Sense*

Lost causes have always been the best challenge to the U.S.A. They are the causes in which we usually achieve our greatest successes.[28]

September 23, 1941, "My Day"

We can't take it for granted that we are the only trustworthy people in the world & we must believe in other people's intelligence & good intentions if we expect them to believe in us. That doesn't mean that we need to be weak either.[29]

February 28, 1943, letter to her daughter Anna

[Y]oung America likes the element of competition in whatever it does.[30]

March 8, 1943, "My Day"

You are an American whether your features are those of a Japanese, whether you have Italian or German ancestry, are born or bred in this country, or are naturalized. You are an American and you take pride in "the American Idea," which claims you as its own when you subscribe to the Constitution and the Bill of Rights. We are Americans all.[31]

October 9, 1943, "My Day," reaction to wartime fear of immigrants from Axis countries

I came back from months on fighting fronts, proud of our achievements. We're got the best army, marines & navy & fliers in the world, the best equipped & fed & paid services. . . . To my surprise I find discouragement, sour faces. My Wall St. friends wail over taxes, my sporting friends over liquor & gas, farmers clamor for high prices, labor for higher wages, so I can't figure out who's doing this wonderful job at home that makes this marvelous job possible overseas & I'm forced to conclude it's the Administration & that man Roosevelt.[32]

November 30, 1943, letter to Joseph P. Lash

No matter what happens to us we seem to come bobbing up again ready to cope with the new situation.[33]

February 26, 1944, "My Day"

This country of ours is unique because we have always expected every generation of young people to do better than their parents.[34]

April 17, 1944, "My Day"

It is a traditional American feeling that we do not have to worry about understanding other people's prejudices and customs, since we can go our own way. With hard work, we expect to get along regardless of what happens to others.[35]

September 28, 1945, "My Day"

Being a strong nation and having the greatest physical, mental and spiritual strength today, gives us a tremendous responsibility. We cannot use our strength to coerce, but if we are big enough, I think we can lead, but it will require great vision and understanding on our part.[36]

November 20, 1945, letter to President Truman

The American way of life means to me freedom to hear all sides of a question; to state my opinion even where the question concerns my government and its officials. It means to me the right of association with people I desire to join with for work or for pleasure. It means belief in civil liberties and an effort to see that they are equal for all people within my country and that opportunity is open to all on an equal basis.[37]

February 2, 1948, letter to a journalist

We are proud people, conscious of our greatness, and yet our traditions of simplicity are important to us. We want dignity but no false pomp and show.[38]

May 18, 1949, "My Day"

It's too easy to take our freedom and individual liberty for granted. We are the strongest democracy in the world, and therefore I believe we have a responsibility to show other nations the great benefits we enjoy because of our form of government. We should not forget the courage and determination it took to declare ourselves independent.[39]

Circa 1950–59

A number of people still think of the United States as being overwhelmingly English, Protestant, and white. This erroneous idea influences their whole outlook.[40]

Circa 1950–59

[N]o one likes the rich uncle who flaunts his wealth in the face of your poverty; who will help you, perhaps—but on his own terms; who will send you to college, if you like—but only to the college of his choice. This, of course, is not a fair description of our attitude but, nevertheless, fair or not, it is the way many see us.[41]

Circa 1953, *India and the Awakening East*

Americans, you see, are not afraid to dive into the unknown. They can surprise the world when they want to.[42]

Circa 1953–54

[T]he primary aim of a nation is no longer to learn to die for one's country. It is more difficult, but far more necessary, to learn to live for one's country.[43]

February 27, 1961, "My Day"

We started from scratch, every American an immigrant who came because he wanted change. *Why are we now afraid to change?*[44]

Circa 1963, *Tomorrow Is Now*

On the American Dream

The American Dream can no more remain static than can the American nation. What I am trying to point out is that we cannot any longer take an old approach to world problems.[45]

Circa 1961, *The Autobiography of Eleanor Roosevelt*

The American Dream is never entirely realized.[46]

Circa 1961, *The Autobiography of Eleanor Roosevelt*

Eleanor Roosevelt with soldiers on the White House lawn, June 12, 1943. Courtesy of the Franklin D. Roosevelt Library and Museum.

3 ✳ On History, War, and Peace

Eleanor Roosevelt excelled in history as an Allenswood student. Later as a teacher at the Todhunter School in New York City, she taught her history, contemporary events, and literature students to make connections between the past and present. Her philosophy was "to seize all opportunities, however unpromising, to make all history and literature and the seemingly barren study of the machinery of government somehow akin to the things the pupils are doing in their daily life."[1]

During World War I, ER volunteered, organized, and managed accounts for several organizations including divisions of the U.S. Navy and the Red Cross. When faced with inadequate care of shell-shocked soldiers at St. Elizabeth's Hospital in Washington, D.C., she lobbied the secretary of the interior to ensure sufficient funding.[2]

Between wars, she spoke out against militarism and supported the nation's peace movements, penning articles like: "Because the War Idea Is Obsolete" (1935) and "War! What the Women of America Can Do to Prevent It" (1939). But when the Japanese attacked Pearl Harbor, she fully supported the nation's entry into World War II.

ER served briefly as the deputy director to the Office of Civilian Defense, but resigned from the unpaid position after five months because of opposition from those who complained the position gave her too much power. Unable to officially serve, she supported the war effort in her writing, declaring "The war is our war."[3]

Not content to sit at home with her four sons in the military, ER visited defense plants and encouraged women to fill the job vacancies of deployed servicemen. She also supported the Women's Army Auxiliary Corps, a volunteer organization of women supporting American troops stateside and overseas.

In the fall of 1942, Queen Elizabeth invited her to England. ER later visited Allied troops in the South Pacific. Criticized at home for traveling during wartime, she was heralded by the soldiers. Far away from the comforts of home, they appreciated her concern and down-to-earth advice. Admiral William Halsey, who originally opposed her coming, marveled at ER's bravery and willingness to endure hardship; "She alone accomplished more good than any other person who passed through my area."[4]

As the Second World War played out, ER expressed her opinions. She sympathized with isolationists and conscientious objectors, but felt their naivety undermined the war effort. She personally opposed Japanese-American internment camps, but did not say so publicly.[5] The harrowing stories of Holocaust survivors made her an advocate for refugees. And though she was initially relieved that the atomic bombs at Hiroshima and Nagasaki ended the war, she soon realized that the weapons could result in the wholesale destruction of humanity.

On History

The civilization of Rome came to an end because individual citizens lost faith in each other.[6]

Circa 1933, *It's Up to the Women*

If we have learned anything from history it is that vindictiveness does not lead to greater happiness, either to the victim or the conqueror.[7]

February 7, 1939, White House press conference

In the history of every country, men have lost their heads for liberty and their hearts for love, and without such men we would have no civilization today.[8]

October 23, 1942, "My Day"

Perhaps to deal with the present, one should not only have knowledge, but a real feeling for the men and circumstances of the past.[9]

February 13, 1943, "My Day"

The value of history lies almost entirely in the insight which it gives to us as to what things in civilization have really had enduring value.[10]

July 31, 1943, "My Day"

From history we learn what in government, in the sciences, in social development, has made people happier. Dates or facts of one kind or another do not matter. What is important is the knowledge from the past as to how best to proceed in the future for the greater happiness of mankind.[11]

July 31, 1943, "My Day"

I believe strongly that the past must never govern the future, I also believe that we must have the past in mind to help us shape the future.[12]

September 3, 1946, keynote address to the New York Democratic State Convention

Each generation supposes that the world is simpler for the one before it.[13]

Circa 1960, *You Learn by Living*

Today we have achieved so much more, in many ways, than our ancestors imagined that sometimes we forget that they dreamed not just for us but for mankind.[14]

Circa 1961, *The Autobiography of Eleanor Roosevelt*

It is essential, above all, that in making history we do not forget to learn by history, to see our mistakes as well as our successes, our weaknesses as well as our strengths.[15]

Circa 1963, *Tomorrow Is Now*

One thing I believe profoundly: *We make our own history.* The course of history is directed by the choices we make and our choices grow out of the ideas, the beliefs, the values, the dreams of the people. It is not so much the powerful leaders that determine our destiny as the much more powerful influence of the combined voices of the people themselves.[16]

Circa 1963, *Tomorrow Is Now*

All big changes in human history have been arrived at slowly and through many compromises.[17]

Circa 1925

On Prohibition

When this law went into effect I confess I looked to it with great hopes. But when I see the terrible things that have grown out of it, such as graft and bootlegging, one begins to wonder about it.[18]

November 9, 1932, *New York Times*

No matter what the legislation, I myself do not drink anything with alcoholic content but that is purely an individual thing. I should not dream of imposing my own conviction on other people as long as they live up to the law of our land.[19]

April 3, 1933, White House press conference

We tried a compulsory law against the liquor traffic once, and all we got from it was worse liquor, more lawbreakers and, if anything, more drunkards than ever.[20]

Circa 1946, *If You Ask Me*

On the Great Depression

At almost stated intervals the pendulum swings, and so far the American people have each time solved their problems. And solve them we will again, but not without earnest consultation and reasoning together.[21]

August 1933, *Woman's Home Companion*

On the Works Progress Administration (WPA)

[The] WPA was necessary, but it was not a subsidy. [The] main purposes of the relief program in this country were met and met certainly at a far lower cost than starvation would have brought to our people as a whole.[22]

November 26, 1943, "My Day"

On the Red Scare and McCarthyism

I am ashamed of the fear we have allowed to be put over us, so that when somebody says that a particular group is Communists, we don't even take the trouble to find out how many are Communists. We are afraid to have anything to do with them. It is too foolish.[23]

November 1938, speech before the New York State Conference of the National Youth Administration

Like so many other countries of the world, we are seizing upon the fear of Communism as a good excuse for attacking anything we do not like.[24]

April 20, 1940, *Liberty*

The Un-American Activities Committee seems to me to be better for a police state than for the USA.[25]

October 29, 1947, "My Day"

I have never liked the idea of an Un-American Activities Committee. I have always thought that a strong democracy should stand by its fundamental beliefs and that a citizen of the United States should be considered innocent until he is proved guilty.[26]

October 29, 1947, "My Day"

I know the danger of communism. . . . I despise the control they insist on holding over men's minds. And that is why I despise what Senator McCarthy has done, for he would use the same methods of fear to control all thought that is not according to his own pattern—in our free country.[27]

August 29, 1952, "My Day"

On War

If we are to do away with the war idea, one of the first steps would be to do away with all possibility of private profit.[28]

Circa 1935, "Because the War Idea Is Obsolete"

It does not matter very much which side you fight on in any war. The effects are just the same whether you win or whether you lose.[29]

Circa 1935, "Because the War Idea Is Obsolete"

The more we kill, the more casual we become about human life.[30]

February 28, 1936, "My Day"

I hope the day will come when all that inventing and mechanical genius will be used for other purposes.[31]

March 13, 1936, "My Day," on viewing a Douglas bomber

Most of us are taught as children to count to 30 before we open our mouths when we were angry, and that same lesson should apply to nations.[32]

March 18, 1936, "My Day"

[A]ll wars eventually act as boomerangs and the victor suffers as much as the vanquished.[33]

February 7, 1939, "My Day"

It is impossible, of course, to be at war and to keep freedom of the press and freedom of speech and freedom of assembly. They disappear automatically.[34]

March 14, 1940, speech to the Chicago Civil Liberties Committee

[W]e cannot neglect the welfare of our children in a time of war and expect to have a future worth fighting for.[35]

March 12, 1942, "My Day"

There is no excuse for the bloodshed, the sacrifices, and the tears which the world as a whole is now enduring, unless we build a new worthwhile world.[36]

July 4, 1942, *Saturday Review of Literature*

War is no respecter of persons and sorrow comes to all, high and low.[37]

August 27, 1942, "My Day"

Even though I never can quite rejoice in the loss of any human life, I can't help being happy each time we have a victory, knowing that if we destroy ships and supply bases and factories faster than the enemy replaces them, the war will be over that much more quickly.[38]

March 8, 1943, "My Day"

How many men there are today whose little children will have to learn to know them after their babyhood is over! This is just another sacrifice made in this war. It may seem insignificant, and yet robs both father and child of something never to be recaptured.[39]

April 20, 1943, "My Day"

I wish that out of this war might come to us a truer evaluation of the worth of human beings and far less interest in the labels of race and religion.[40]

June 19, 1943, "My Day"

We lost the peace in the last war, and perhaps my nation was partly to blame, but I doubt if any nation was really prepared then to think and act in a way that would have united the world.[41]

September 6, 1943, *Morning Bulletin* (Rockhampton, Queensland, Australia)

[W]ar is a ruthless business. It cannot be conducted along humanitarian lines. The sooner our pacifists and church groups realize this and bend their efforts to winning the war, the better it will be for the children of the world.[42]

March 6, 1944, "My Day"

Men on the field of battle and men and women at home are going through daily crucifixion, and only faith and hope can make their victory sure.[43]

April 10, 1944, "My Day"

War, however, is never a civilized proceeding.[44]

August 16, 1944, "My Day"

We have to remember that in the future we will want to keep before our children what this war was really like. It is so easy to forget; and then, for the younger generation, the heroism and the glamour remains, while the dirt, the hardships, the horror of death and the sorrow fade somewhat from their consciousness.[45]

June 5, 1945, "My Day"

War is the result of failures of human beings and not of their successes.[46]

Circa 1946, *If You Ask Me*

No one won the last war, and no one will win the next war.[47]

March 22, 1948, letter to President Truman

I had a feeling that I might be saying good-bye for the last time. It was sort of a precursor of what it would be like if your children were killed and never to come back. Life had to go on and you had to do what was required of you, but something inside you quietly died.[48]

Circa 1949, *This I Remember*, on saying farewell to her sons as they went off to war

The loss of a generation makes itself felt acutely twenty-five years later, when many men who would have been leaders are just not there to lead.[49]

Circa 1949, *This I Remember*

Not the people, but governments, make war. And then they persuade the people that it is in a good cause, the cause of their own defense.[50]

October 5, 1957, "My Day"

On World War II

[W]e have only postponed a war unless we are prepared to let Hitler and his ideas dominate Europe.[51]

October 3, 1938, letter to her daughter, reacting to the appeasement policy

It seems like a completely changed world.[52]

December 11, 1941, letter to Lorena Hickok, reaction to the bombing of Pearl Harbor

We are beginning to realize, I think, as the days go on, that this war is on a vaster scale than anything which we have ever dreamed of before.[53]

January 3, 1942, "My Day"

Perhaps it is good for us to have to face disaster, because we have been so optimistic and almost arrogant in our expectation of constant success. Now we shall have to find within us the courage to meet defeat and fight right on to victory.[54]

February 17, 1942, "My Day," reaction to the fall of Singapore

The only way I can see to get the maximum service out of our citizens, is to draft us all and to tell us all where we can be most useful and where our work is needed. So long as we are left to volunteer, we are bound to waste our capacities and to do things which are not necessary.[55]

March 10, 1942, "My Day"

The Queen showed me her own destroyed rooms here & all windows are out! It is a curious place but the people give you a sense of unity.[56]

October 23, 1942, letter to Lorena Hickok, on her London visit

Our most vivid impression I think is what a blackout of an entire city means. You get a curious feeling over here that nothing but people count.[57]

November 5, 1942, letter to Lorena Hickok, on the London blackouts

One can only pray that it will dawn upon Hitler that the Lord is not patient forever and that he who puts other people to death by the sword, is often meted out the same fate.[58]

December 5, 1942, "My Day"

[W]e should make it a prerequisite that the older people who are responsible are promptly sent out to die in these frontier battles. Why should the young always be expendable for the mistakes of the old?[59]

January 23, 1943, "My Day," reaction to inadequately supplied soldiers

These boys break your heart, they're so young & so tired. Malaria is almost as bad as bullets. They are hardly out of [the] hospital before they are at the Red Cross Clubs & dances & they laugh at everything. I take my hat off to this young generation & hope we don't let them down.[60]

September 1, 1943, letter to Lorena Hickok, on Allied soldiers in Auckland, New Zealand

This is a war of the people as a whole. We, at home, are just as much a part of it as the soldiers in the field.[61]

October 5, 1943, "My Day"

This war is being fought for Four great Freedoms—Freedom of Religion, Freedom from Want, Freedom from Fear, and Freedom of Expression; in the press, by assembly, and in any way that information reaches the people.[62]

October 28, 1943, "My Day"

We are a fortunate nation, nevertheless. War is not on our doorsteps. We are not living under enemy rule. We haven't had to see our boys taken off in labor drafts, our girls taken out of our villages and cities to even worse fates. If that happened to us we would understand the looks that we find on the faces of some refugees from Poland, or Czechoslovakia, or Holland or Norway. Oh, the world is a sad place to live in these days, and God grant we learn our lesson. It is not enough to hate war. We must have power to build for peace and we must be willing to make the sacrifices which that entails.[63]

February 9, 1944, "My Day"

It is hard to believe that the beaches of France, which we once knew, are now places from which, in days to come, boys in hospitals over here will tell us that they have returned. They may never go beyond the water or the beach, but all their lives, perhaps, they will bear the marks of this day. At that, they will be fortunate, for many others won't return.[64]

June 7, 1944, "My Day," on the D-Day invasion

Paris has always been a symbol, and now . . . it is again a city where Frenchmen are free.[65]

August 26, 1944, "My Day," on the liberation of Paris

[E]very one of us knows quite well that once the bombs dropped on our soil at Pearl Harbor, the war was no longer a *foreign* war, but was a war in defense of our own country. Had we not fought on distant shores, we would soon have fought on the shores of the United States.[66]

November 21, 1944, "My Day"

There must be joy, of course, in the hearts of the peoples whom the Nazis conquered and who are now free again. Freedom without bread, however, has little meaning.[67]

May 9, 1945, "My Day," reaction to V.E. Day

I cannot feel a spirit of celebration today. I am glad that our men are no longer going to be shot at and killed in Europe, but the war in the Pacific still goes on. Men are dying there, even as I write.[68]

May 9, 1945, "My Day," reaction to V.E. Day

There is a quiet rejoicing that men are no longer bringing death to each other throughout the world. There is great happiness, too, in the knowledge that someday, soon, many of those we love will be at home again to give all they have to the rebuilding of a peaceful world.[69]

August 15, 1945, "My Day," on V-J day

[T]he war is over. We will not be engaged in the business of killing each other. Mass murder is ended, and we can rejoice.[70]

August 18, 1945, "My Day"

On Nazism

The Nazi psychology is a strange one, because fear and suffering do not create love and loyalty.[71]

September 25, 1942, "My Day"

Where the theory of a master race is accepted, there is danger to all progress in civilization.[72]

April 30, 1945, "My Day"

On Conscientious Objectors

I found it very hard during the war to have much patience with the young men who were conscientious objectors. . . . [I]t was hard to keep down the feeling that they were exercising this freedom to live up to their religious beliefs at the expense of some other boy's sacrifice.[73]

September 5, 1945, "My Day"

On Women and War

In our emphasis on defense projects, I feel it important to remember that girls as well as boys can be fitted for defense work. They, too, must have training in order to earn their livings and live better than they have done in the past.[74]

May 23, 1941, "My Day"

No woman can do a greater service today in the war effort than to devote herself to seeing that her home meets, to the limit, the demands made by the government.[75]

July 11, 1942, "My Day"

[I]f the war goes on long enough, and women are patient, opportunity will come knocking at their doors. However, there is just a chance that this is not a time when women should be patient. We are in a war and we need to fight it with all our ability and every weapon possible. Women pilots, in this particular case, are a weapon waiting to be used.[76]

September 1, 1942, "My Day"

Life in the armed services is hard and uncomfortable, but I think women can stand up under that type of living just as well as men.[77]

October 15, 1943, "My Day"

On the Atomic Bomb

We now have the discovery I'm told which [FDR] feared Germany would have first but I gather no one wants to use it for its destructive power is so great that no one knows where it might stop.[78]

June 25, 1944, letter to Joseph P. Lash

This new discovery cannot be ignored. We have only two alternative choices: destruction and death—or construction and life![79]

August 8, 1945, "My Day," reaction to the bombing of Hiroshima

All the world has a right to share in the beneficence which may grow from its proper development.[80]

August 15, 1945, "My Day"

If we had not taken the gamble of discovery, we would have taken the greater gamble of destruction in the event that Germany won in the race.[81]

August 27, 1945, "My Day"

Now we face the fact that scientists have made it possible for us to do such a successful job of exterminating other human beings that, unless we stop doing it in the mass way we call war, the human race will commit suicide.[82]

September 5, 1945, "My Day"

Every man, every woman—everywhere—must grow up knowing that since this discovery of how to use atomic energy for destruction, annihilation faces them unless they learn to live in a peaceful world and to allow the policing of the world to be done by an international security agency.[83]

September 25, 1945, "My Day"

Once a weapon is discovered, it will always be used by those who are in desperate straits.[84]

September 25, 1945, "My Day"

The day we found the secret of the atomic bomb, we closed one phase of civilization and entered upon another.[85]

September 25, 1945, "My Day"

[U]nless we remove any reason for its destructive use, there may be no future generations![86]

October 3, 1945, "My Day"

I think that if the atomic bomb did nothing more, it scared the people to the point where they realized that either they must do something about preventing war or there is a chance that there might be a morning when we would not wake up.[87]

January 6, 1946, news conference aboard the RMS *Queen Elizabeth*

It seems to me that the discovery of this latest bomb has actually outlawed the use of atomic bombs. The power of destruction is so great that unless we face the fact that no one in the world can possibly use it and therefore it must be outlawed as a weapon, we risk putting an end to civilization.[88]

April 16, 1954, "My Day," on the hydrogen bomb

On Soldiers

I shall never forget my feeling of horror when I learned that the Army had actually been ordered to evict the veterans. . . . This one incident shows what fear can make people do.[89]

Circa 1949, *This I Remember*, on the Bonus Marchers

It is a curious thing to me, that older people seem so often to accept with complacency these young armies. I rebel, and yet I know an army must be young.[90]

January 28, 1942, "My Day"

[E]very American soldier I see is a friend from home.[91]

November 6, 1942, "My Day"

They will know that their contribution was the greatest to the generations of the future and we shall stand humbly before them.[92]

July 30, 1943, "My Day"

[T]he Army's job is really not complete. It took men and turned them into soldiers, and so it has a responsibility to turn them back into good citizens—not unhappy and disillusioned human beings.[93]

June 17, 1944, "My Day"

They can make us friends in the world or they can create for us new enemies.[94]

October 29, 1945, "My Day"

I can subscribe to universal military training. A year spent in service and education which would emphasize the responsibility of a citizen in a democracy to his country would seem to me of value to both men and women.[95]

September 2, 1947, "My Day," advocating universal military service

On Japanese-American Internment Camps

I am confident that the government will do everything possible to make the evacuation as decent and as comfortable as possible, and it will provide protection against vigilantes and misguided private citizens.[96]

April 7, 1942, *New York Times*

On the Holocaust

These mass removals, where people are treated like animals and not like human beings, are so horrible to contemplate, that one can only hope that at a certain point feelings become numb and suffering ceases to be acute.[97]

October 25, 1941, "My Day," on the expulsion of Jews from Germany to Poland and Russia

Every woman and child taken from that village to a concentration camp will carry in their hearts a hatred which can never turn into tolerance for the people or the system.[98]

June 12, 1942, "My Day," reaction to the massacre in Lidice, Czechoslovakia

These children present a different problem, for many of them will never see their parents again, since they have been left behind in concentration camps in various European countries.[99]

May 14, 1943, "My Day," on child refugees

[The Warsaw ghetto uprising][100] makes one ashamed that a civilized race anywhere in the world could treat other human beings in such a manner.[101]

June 8, 1944, "My Day"

Something must have happened that we know nothing about to turn people who were highly educated and civilized into sadists who enjoy seeing other human beings suffer.[102]

April 28, 1945, "My Day," on the perpetrators of the Holocaust

It would be pleasant to close our eyes and ears now and say: "These things could never be. Human beings could not do such things, and therefore we will not believe them or listen to them." That would be an easy way out because we would not have to decide how we could prevent any recurrence in the future, in any part of the world.[103]

May 2, 1945, "My Day"

[T]hose who have suffered under the Nazis—no matter what their nationality or religion—are not our enemies or the enemies of the Allied nations, and should not be treated as such.[104]

September 24, 1945, "My Day," reaction to detention of Holocaust survivors

On the Postwar Period

If we give people bread, we may build friendship among the peoples of the world; and we will never have peace without friendship around the world. This is the time for a long look ahead. This is the time for us all to decide where we go from here.[105]

May 9, 1945, "My Day"

We have spent tremendous sums on the war, most of it for destruction. Even a minute percentage of that sum spent now for constructive purposes would keep us from having mass unemployment. If at the same time we raise the standard of home environment, we will be doing something of double value to the nation.[106]

August 16, 1945, "My Day"

The whole social structure of Europe is crumbling and we might as well face the fact that leadership must come from us or it will inevitably come from Russia.[107]

March 1, 1946, letter to President Truman

On the Cold War

There is only one answer to these fears, and that is a belief that the Soviet Union and the United States, as well as the United Nations as a whole, can live peacefully together—and a determination on the part of their people to do so.[108]

August 11, 1945, "My Day"

On Peace

[I]f peace is going to come about in the world, the way to start is by getting a better understanding between individuals. From this germ a better understanding between groups will grow.[109]

Circa 1938, "This Troubled World"

We will have to want peace, want it enough to pay for it, pay for it in our own behavior and in material ways. We will have to want it enough to overcome our lethargy and go out and find all those in our countries who want it as much as we do.[110]

Circa 1938, "This Troubled World"

Negotiation, mediation or arbitration are just words, but any one of them if put into practice now by people who really want to keep peace, might mean life instead of death to hundreds of thousands.[111]

August 26, 1939, "My Day"

A breach of peace anywhere is a menace to peace everywhere.[112]

October 10, 1939, White House press conference

Peace is something we want to work for, day in and day out, but we want to work for it with the knowledge that only justice keeps the people of the world at peace.[113]

December 9, 1942, "My Day"

Trying to obtain world peace is enlightened self-interest.[114]

December 16, 1943, "My Day"

Peace will not be built, however, by people with bitterness in their hearts.[115]

January 7, 1944, "My Day"

I do not think there can be any peace in weakness; I am sure it lies in strength, but I think strength must be used in an understanding and cooperative spirit. Somehow, the selfishness of human beings must be controlled so that peace may be strengthened by justice and a sense of security throughout the world.[116]

September 13, 1944, "My Day"

[P]eace is no longer a question of something we hope to attain in the future. It is an absolutely vital necessity to the continuation of our civilization on earth.[117]

October 6, 1945, "My Day"

If only we all would realize that every time we allow ourselves to have an unkind and bitter thought about another human being we add to these tensions and put another nail in the coffin of world peace.[118]

October 12, 1945, "My Day"

It takes just as much determination to work for peace as it does to win a war.[119]

November 16, 1945, address to Roosevelt College

[I]ndividuals should want peace, should care about other human beings all over the world regardless of race, creed, or color, and should be determined that they will not seek for purely personal advantage, but will see for mutual advantage.[120]

Circa 1946, *If You Ask Me*

Peace has to begin within each individual's heart and has to be lived by each of us every day.[121]

August 30, 1947, "My Day"

And I don't feel that just "sweetness and light" by itself is going to win a just peace. I think we need clear facing of facts and holding on to our own ideas, and trying to bring the world to a sense of strength in all ways.[122]

June 1948, *Christian Register*

For it isn't enough to talk of peace. One must believe it. And it isn't enough to believe in it. One must work at it.[123]

November 11, 1951, Voice of America broadcast

To achieve peace we must recognize the historic truth that we can no longer live apart from the rest of the world. We must also recognize the fact that peace, like freedom, is not won once and for all. It is fought for daily, in many small acts, and is the result of many individual efforts.[124]

Summer of 1952, address to the United Nations Convention

[W]e must learn to live together or at some point we are apt to die together.[125]

January 22, 1959, "My Day"

Eleanor Roosevelt visiting the Horuji Temple in Nara, Japan, June 7, 1953. Courtesy of the Franklin D. Roosevelt Library and Museum.

4 ❈ On Religion

Eleanor Roosevelt was a lifelong member of the Episcopal Church. In her youth, Sunday was a day for religious services and contemplation, and she was not permitted to play games or read secular books. Despite these restrictions, ER fondly remembered singing religious hymns around the piano on Sunday evenings.[1]

When she married and became a mother, she became responsible for her children's religious education. She instructed them in Bible lessons at home and brought them to church, though she sometimes resented her husband's decision to play golf instead.[2]

ER lived by the standards and moral precepts of Protestant Christianity, but she was open-minded about other denominations and faiths. She believed in the separation of church and state as one of the nation's core values. Though ER supported school-based prayer and Bible reading, she opposed federal funding for parochial schools. As a result, in 1949, Cardinal Francis Spellman accused her of being anti-Catholic. Their heated letters contributed to the already tense 1949 presidential campaign. They later reconciled during a meeting at Hyde Park.[3]

On Religion

The fundamental, vital thing which must be alive in each human consciousness is the religious teaching that we cannot live for ourselves alone and that as long as we are here on this earth we are all of us brothers, regardless of race, creed, or color.[4]

December 1932, *Forum*

We are a mixed nation of many peoples and many religions, but most of us would accept the life of Christ as a pattern for our democratic way of life, and Christ taught love and never hate.[5]

July 14, 1943, "My Day"

Christ to me is a man (divine or not, what matters?) who fought a fight in his day almost single handed, but everyone who takes up the fight is of the same kind.[6]

November 11, 1943, letter to Joseph P. Lash

Each man may have his own religion; the church is merely the outward and visible symbol of the longing of the human soul for something to which he can aspire and which he desires beyond his own strength to achieve.[7]

Circa 1940, "The Moral Basis of Democracy"

How marvelously arrogant we all are in our use of the name of the Lord. Each one of us, feeling sure that the Lord is with us, proclaims the righteousness of his cause.[8]

January 2, 1941, "My Day"

[N]o matter what we human beings do that is wrong or stupid, the power that is God believes eventually we may grow better.[9]

April 15, 1941, "My Day"

[I] am very apt to be rather superficial in my knowledge of religious subjects. I am afraid that my reading of the Bible and the New Testament has been confined often to sections which I like particularly and not to sections which are particularly concerned with the reasons for my beliefs.[10]

October 10, 1941, "My Day"

Religion to me is simply the conviction that all human beings must hold some belief in a power greater than themselves, and that whatever their religious belief may be, it must move them to live better in this world and to approach whatever the future holds with serenity.[11]

October 1941, *Ladies' Home Journal*

The important thing is neither your nationality nor the religion you profess, but how your faith translated itself in your life.[12]

September 23, 1943, "My Day"

Christ was a great psychiatrist. He said we had to be like little children because he knew just thinking alone never solved the riddle which at some time preoccupies us all.[13]

June 3, 1944, letter to Joseph P. Lash

If only the teachings of Christ were accepted as the actual code by which we lived, how different our world would be! There would be no labor-management problems in industry, no racial or religious hatreds, no wars to bring sorrow to men, women and children throughout the world. I wonder if it is too much to expect that Christ's ethics will someday govern the actions of human beings.[14]

November 25, 1944, "My Day"

The life of Christ is the symbol of the perfect kind of love, the love which should rule the world.[15]

December 25, 1944, "My Day"

It does very little good to believe something unless you tell your friends and associates of your beliefs.[16]

May 7, 1945, "My Day"

The churches will have to take a stand against unthinking and un-Christian prejudices. They will have to develop among the people a greater sense of responsibility for the conditions existing in society.[17]

August 8, 1946, "My Day"

In one way, of course, the Adam and Eve story is true as an allegory, but when taught without interpretation, as many children learn it, it is not true.[18]

Circa 1946, *If You Ask Me*

Almost any other religion [in addition to Christianity], if you lived up to the ideals of the founders, would lead you to what might be termed a revolutionary way of living. No political revolutions would be necessary if religion become a vital part of everyday life.[19]

Circa 1946, *If You Ask Me*

Also, I would have been delighted to see in the preamble [of the United Nations Declaration of Human Rights] a paragraph alluding to the Supreme Power. I knew very well, however, there were many men around the table who would violently be opposed to naming God, and I did not want it put to a vote because I thought for those of us who are Christians it would be rather difficult to have God defeated in a vote.[20]

December 10, 1948, "My Day"

I can assure you that I have no prejudice. I understand the beliefs of the Roman Catholic Church very well. I happen to be a Protestant and I prefer my own church, but that does not make me feel that any one has any less right to believe as his own convictions guide him.[21]

July 23, 1949, letter to Cardinal Francis Spellman

[C]hristianity is the basis for real democracy.[22]

September 27, 1950, "My Day"

Trying to make Stalin and the Communist party take the place of God has not succeeded even with many Russian people, and it seems to me that it would be almost impossible to wipe out religion by offering Communism in its place unless people had already lost their faith in their religion.[23]

September 1953, *McCall's Magazine*

I think suffering strengthens anyone's religion, because there is a feeling that one needs strength beyond one's own capacity to carry a burden, whether it be a physical, mental or spiritual burden.[24]

August 1954, *McCall's Magazine*

[I]f, in the course of the years, I have gained any wisdom whatsoever, it is the wisdom to know that the Kingdom of God must come on earth through the efforts of human beings and that war in the atomic age will simply mean annihilation, certainly not evolution.[25]

September 13, 1947, "My Day"

For just as the Soviet Union has made a religion out of a political creed—communism—so, by a kind of reverse twist, the followers of Islam have made their religion an integral and controlling part of their political life.[26]

Circa 1953, *India and the Awakening East*

Religious freedom cannot just be Protestant freedom. It must be freedom for all religions.[27]

September 20, 1960, "My Day"

Like all our other freedoms, this freedom from religious-group pressure must be constantly defended.[28]

Circa 1961, *The Autobiography of Eleanor Roosevelt*

On Religion in Schools

But I have never been able to see why there was anything to prevent any school from opening with the Lord's Prayer and a hymn, in exactly the same way as they salute the flag. . . . There is no reason for fear in the case of a group that does not believe in any religion. They can stay in the room. It doesn't do them any harm.[29]

January 22, 1940, White House press conference

There is no real reason why every school should not teach every child that one of the important aspects of our life is its spiritual side. It might be possible to devise a prayer that all denominations could say and it certainly ought to be possible to read certain verses from the Bible every day. It probably would do children no harm to learn to know some of the writings of the great religious leaders who have lead other great religious movements.[30]

July 15, 1949, "My Day"

I believe there should be freedom for every child to be educated in his own religion. In public schools it should be taught that the spiritual side of life is most important.... The real religious teaching of any child must be done in his own church and in his own home.[31]

July 23, 1949, letter to Cardinal Spellman

Anyone who knows history, particularly the history of Europe, will, I think, recognize that the domination of education or of government by any one particular religious faith is never a happy arrangement for the people.[32]

July 24, 1949, response to criticism by Cardinal Spellman

On the Separation of Church and State

The separation of church and state is extremely important to any of us who hold the original traditions of our nation. To change these traditions by changing our traditional attitude toward public education would be harmful.[33]

June 23, 1949, "My Day"

The recognition of any church as a temporal power puts that church in a different position from any of the other churches and while we are now only hearing from the Protestant groups, the Moslems may one day wake up to this and make an equal howl. For us who take a firm stand on the separation of church and state, the recognition of temporal power seems inconsistent.[34]

January 29, 1952, letter to President Harry Truman

On Death and Life after Death

Death should be calm and serene when work is done and well done, there is nothing to regret either for those who go or for those who stay behind.[35]

April 22, 1936, "My Day"

One of the sad things about growing old must be to see one's friends depart on the greatest of all adventures, and to find the world growing lonely. It is perhaps this gradual feeling of detachment, however, that makes it easier for us older people to cross the last bar with apparent ease and equanimity.[36]

November 22, 1944, "My Day"

Perhaps nature is our best assurance of immortality.[37]

April 26, 1945, "My Day"

One does not weep for those who die, particularly when they have lived a full life. And I doubt in any case whether the gauge of love and sorrow is in the tears that are shed in the first days of mourning.

People who remain with you in your daily life, even though they are no longer physically present, who are frequently in your mind, often mentioned, part of your laughter, part of your joy—they are the people you really miss. They are the people from whom you are never quite separated. You do not need to walk heavily all your life to really miss people.[38]

April 14, 1953, "My Day"

When you cease to make a contribution, you begin to die.[39]

February 19, 1960, letter to Mr. Horne

I happen to think that a belief in God is all that is necessary for the acceptance of death, since you know that death, like life, is part of God's plan.[40]

Circa 1960, *You Learn by Living*

I have no idea if there is an afterlife or not, but I'll find out soon enough.[41]

Date unknown

Eleanor Roosevelt holding a copy of the Declaration of Human Rights, November 1949.
Courtesy of the Franklin D. Roosevelt Library and Museum.

5 ✳ On Freedoms, Rights, and Threats to Them

To Eleanor Roosevelt, freedom was the core of American democracy. Specifically, she advanced the Four Freedoms from her husband's January 1941 Message to Congress: freedom of speech and expression, freedom of religion, freedom from want, and freedom from fear, for all citizens. She further believed that all citizens must have the right to disagree.

In 1946, President Harry Truman appointed ER to serve as a delegate to the United Nations, where she was appointed to chair the drafting committee charged with establishing a Universal Declaration of Human Rights. Under her guidance, the charter promoted equal rights regardless of "race, color, sex, language, religion, political or other opinion, national or social origin, property, birth or other status."[1] She considered the Declaration the greatest accomplishment of her life.

On Rights

All through the years we have had to fight for civil liberty, and we know that there are times when the light grows rather dim, and every time that happens democracy is in danger.[2]

March 14, 1940, address to the Chicago Civil Liberties Committee

All human beings are born free and equal in dignity and rights.[3]

Circa 1948, from the Universal Declaration of Human Rights

Where after all do universal human rights begin? In small places, close to home—so close and so small that they cannot be seen on any map of the world. Yet they *are* the world of the individual person: The neighborhood he lives in; the school or college he attends; the factory, farm or office where he works. Such are the places where every man, woman, and child seeks equal justice, equal opportunity, equal dignity without discrimination. Unless these rights have meaning there, they have little meaning anywhere. Without concerted citizen action to uphold them close to home, we shall look in vain for progress in the larger world.[4]

March 27, 1958, speech to the United Nations

On Privacy

Does it ever occur to you that it would be pleasant if no one ever wrote about me? Mrs. Doaks would like a little privacy now & then.[5]

November 18, 1933, letter to Lorena Hickok. "Mrs. Doaks" was an alias.

[N]o one knows when a television camera is turned his way. . . . Unless you are constantly aware that you are under scrutiny you are apt to be caught at unexpected and embarrassing moments.[6]

Circa 1961, *The Autobiography of Eleanor Roosevelt*

I am still taken aback to discover how closely one's most trivial moments are followed in this day of television. It seems as though one can find privacy only within the silence of one's own mind.[7]

Circa 1961, *The Autobiography of Eleanor Roosevelt*

On Freedom

At all times, day by day, we have to continue fighting for freedom of religion, freedom of speech, freedom from fear, and freedom from want—for these are things that must be gained in peace as well as in war.[8]

April 15, 1943, "My Day"

In the democracies of the world, the passion for freedom of speech and of thought is always accentuated when there is an effort anywhere to keep ideas away from people and to prevent them from making their own decisions.[9]

May 11, 1943, "My Day"

Every citizen in this country has a right to our basic freedoms, to justice and to equality of opportunity, and we retain the right to lead our individual lives as we please, but we can only do so if we grant to others the freedoms that we wish for ourselves.[10]

October 16, 1943, *Collier's*

Great power is always dangerous to freedom and unless we share this power with the other nations of the world, and are ever careful to make it of value to the people of the world, we may find ourselves becoming less the defenders of freedom than the custodians of power.[11]

May 30, 1944, "My Day"

I have never been able to see, however, how anyone could resent what people felt or said about you. One might be sorry that in some way one had hurt or offended an individual or a group, but certainly in a free country everyone has a right to an opinion and to the expression of it.[12]

October 20, 1944, "My Day"

[H]uman freedom is a precious thing, and you cannot take it away from people and not feel the result.[13]

November 2, 1945, "My Day," reaction to touring a women's prison

It is obvious that freedom is always conditioned by the amount of ability an individual has to govern himself.[14]

Circa 1946, *If You Ask Me*

Freedom from want means being sure that if you want to work, you can get a job and that that job will pay you sufficient to give you and your family a decent standard of living.[15]

Circa 1946, *If You Ask Me*

It seems to me that if you curtail freedom in any respect, you curtail it sooner or later in every respect.[16]

October 28, 1945, speech to the United Nations General Assembly

I think if we care for the preservation of our liberties we must allow all people, whether we disagree with them or not, to hold meetings and express their views unmolested as long as they do not advocate the overthrow of our government by force.[17]

September 3, 1949, "My Day"

Freedom is not really freedom unless you can differ in thought and in expression of your thought.[18]

January 14, 1952, *Department of State Bulletin*

I'm intensely anxious to preserve the freedom that gives you the right to think and to act and to talk as you please. That I think is essential to happiness and the life of the people.[19]

November 23, 1957, interview by Mike Wallace

Freedom makes a huge requirement of every human being. With freedom comes responsibility. For the person who is unwilling to grow up, the person who does not want to carry his own weight, this is a frightening prospect.[20]

Circa 1960, *You Learn by Living*

[F]or only in freedom can man function completely.[21]

Circa 1960, *The Autobiography of Eleanor Roosevelt*

On Censorship

One thing is sure—none of the arts flourishes on censorship and repression. And by this time it should be evident the American public is capable of doing its own censoring.[22]

October 29, 1947, "My Day"

On Book Burning

Instead of making people pay less attention to what these authors had to say, it made many more people read them, who, perhaps, had never read them before. Their contributions to the thinking of the world are probably far greater than they would have been without Hitler's effort at suppression.[23]

May 11, 1943, "My Day," reaction to the ten-year anniversary of Nazi book burnings

Eleanor Roosevelt working at a soup kitchen during the Depression, 1933. Courtesy of the Franklin D. Roosevelt Library and Museum.

6 ❋ On Work

Eleanor Roosevelt came of age in an era when respectable women might volunteer for a good cause but were discouraged from working outside the home. As a young woman, ER volunteered at the Rivington Street Settlement House. Later, when her husband was assistant secretary to the U.S. Navy, she used her organizational skills to aid World War I soldiers and veterans. During the 1920s, ER was a lobbyist and an organizer for Democratic organizations.

When she became First Lady of New York, she served as her wheelchair-bound husband's eyes and legs, traveling to schools, hospitals, and prisons. She left no corner uninspected, no question unasked, and looked in the cooking pots to ensure menus were accurate.[1] While volunteering was personally fulfilling, ER gained a degree of personal and financial independence in 1927 when she became a teacher at the Todhunter School, a vocation she continued after becoming the First Lady of New York.

While her husband was governor and later president, ER wrote monthly, then daily columns, penned freelance articles for magazines, wrote question-and-answer columns, and published twenty-eight books. She also delivered frequent radio and later television broadcasts. After FDR's death, her lecture tours took her all over the world.

Because she found work personally fulfilling, ER considered the right to work sacred. She supported employment programs and championed equal wages for women. ER sympathized with workers and supported labor unions.

On Work

There is one thing, however, which we can all do, namely, we can make it possible for our children to appreciate what work is.[2]

June 1931, *Parent's Magazine*

It is un-American to say anybody should not work. It is class legislation of the very worst kind to say that a particular class of people can't work.[3]

July 6, 1933, White House press conference

The right to work seems to me as vital a part of our freedom as any right which we may have.[4]

November 1933, *Woman's Home Companion*

Whatever work I am doing is interesting, because it is a game to find time enough to do it.[5]

April 21, 1938, "My Day"

I do not suppose that any really good work is ever lost. Somewhere the seed remains and the influence is felt in the future.[6]

March 14, 1941, "My Day"

There is no one who believes more strongly than I do that play and rest are important in life, but above and beyond everything else, work must be to us all the phase of our lives for which we are most grateful.[7]

September 1, 1941, "My Day"

It is true that machines have taken over the work of human hands to a great extent, but the real problem before us is how to make the work of the machines a benefit to human beings and not a detriment.[8]

August 7, 1941, "My Day"

The things you are not doing are always much more adventurous than your own job.[9]

October 1, 1942, "My Day"

What one has to do usually can be done.[10]

Circa 1944

But my philosophy has been that if you have work to do and do it to the best of your ability you will not have so much time to think about yourself.[11]

Circa 1958, *On My Own*

If you have more projects than you have time for, you are not going to be an unhappy person.[12]

Circa 1960, *You Learn by Living*

It is not more vacation we need—it is more vocation.[13]

Circa 1963, *Tomorrow Is Now*

My experience has been that work is almost the best way to pull oneself out of the depths.[14]

January 11, 1939, letter to Pauline Emmett

On Working in the Home

[M]arriages and the upbringing of children in the home require as well trained a mind and as well-disciplined a character as any other occupation that might be considered a career.[15]

March 29, 1941, "My Day"

Much of what a wife does at home can never be paid for, but she is quite justified in thinking that there is an actual money value to some of the things which she does.[16]

Circa 1946, *If You Ask Me*

I think anything connected with the home is as much the husband's work as the wife's. This silly idea that there is a division in housework seems to me foolish. . . . The kind of man who thinks helping with the dishes is beneath him will also think that helping with the baby is beneath him, and then he certainly is not going to be a very successful father.[17]

Circa 1946, *If You Ask Me*

More people are affected by the occupation of a housewife and mother than are ever touched by a single business, no matter how large it may be.[18]

"My Day," October 17, 1955

On Working Women

There is no reason why we should not have a female Henry Ford. I am hopeful for women in industry. They will have to overcome prejudice, a natural prejudice, which will disappear as soon as they prove themselves capable industrial heads.[19]

November 16, 1930, *New York Times*

A woman, just like a man, may have a great gift for some particular thing. That does not mean that she must give up the joy of marrying and having a home and children.[20]

Circa 1933, *It's Up to the Women*

I think that the freeing of women from household tasks has made them able to leave their babies and their homes and emerge into other fields. That is their greatest achievement in the last 100 years.[21]

January 12, 1941, *New York Times*

I know all the old arguments that a woman is supposed to be dependent on some man and that the man must be paid more because of the people he supports. But it has been proved over and over again that single women not only support themselves, but often other members of their families as well, so I think we should revise our schedules and come more nearly to equality of payment when the same work is performed.[22]

April 19, 1943, "My Day," response to the common practice of paying lower wages to women for the same job

We women should be loyal and generous to each other. We cannot all do the same things, but we can admire other women when they do good work in the occupations which they feel they can undertake.[23]

October 22, 1943, "My Day"

If women do the same work I have always believed that they should receive the same pay.[24]

Circa 1946, *If You Ask Me*

On Unemployment

We seem to forget that the unemployed are individuals, human beings with all the tastes and likes and dislikes and passions we have ourselves. When we meet them as individuals our feeling is entirely different, but as a group we talk about them as though they were so many robots.[25]

April 29, 1936, "My Day"

I often wonder how we can make the more fortunate in this country fully aware of the fact that the problem of the unemployed is not a mechanical one. It is a problem alive and throbbing with human pain.[26]

April 29, 1936, "My Day"

On Business

Business today, with all its complicated ramifications, seems a bit like the Mad Hatter's Tea Party![27]

February 20, 1936, "My Day"

Business complications do strange things to our patriotism and to our ethics![28]

September 20, 1945, "My Day," reaction to a rumored link between Nazi Germany and the Ford Motor Company

On Labor and Unions

To me, organization for labor seems necessary because it is the only protection that the worker has when he feels that he is not receiving just returns for his labor, or that he is working under conditions which he cannot accept as fair. I also feel that dealing with organized labor should benefit the employer and make for better mutual understanding.[29]

March 13, 1941, "My Day"

A union organization fails in its full duty when it loses the ideal which lies back of all unionization. This ideal, it seems to me, is an unselfish interest in those who are not as strong as others in their ability to defend themselves, and in a willingness to suffer to obtain for others the rights you may have already achieved for yourself.[30]

March 13, 1941, "My Day"

Since this is to be the century of the common man, there must be a partnership between those who work with their hands and those who work with their heads. They must all insist on their common interest because they are the workers of the world. They are the mass of people who must control their governments in order to have a chance to build a better life throughout the world.[31]

April 16, 1943, "My Day"

The only thing that can be done to help any workers to obtain proper working conditions and to get better wages is to organize.[32]

Circa 1946, *If You Ask Me*

One of the places where the greatest progress has been made is in unions. I think that is because where men work together they get to know each other better. They cease to be just a colored man, a Jew or a "wop." They are fellow workers and they frequently have to depend on one another.[33]

August 22, 1952, "My Day"

On Strikes

I can't cross a picket line—fair or unfair.[34]

Circa June 1942

There should be no strike. . . . They should voluntarily give it up in wartime.[35]

April 30, 1943, *New York Times*, on the United Mine Workers' strike in Pittsburgh

[E]very employer who forces his employees into a position where they see no way out except to strike is equally guilty with the strikers. I have seen so many condemnations of strikers, but I have seen little recognition that there are always two sides to any dispute.[36]

June 7, 1944, "My Day"

If I cross a picket line I take sides with the employer. If I do not, I take no sides whatever.[37]

Circa 1946, *If You Ask Me*

Desperate men don't strike. During the depression there were few strikes. A strike is a sign of a worker's faith that he can better his condition.[38]

Circa 1960, *You Learn by Living*

Eleanor Roosevelt in London, December 1951. Courtesy of the Franklin D. Roosevelt Library and Museum.

7 ☀ On Money and Economics

Eleanor Roosevelt was raised as a member of the upper-class elite during an era of conspicuous consumption. Since her family members squandered money, ER paid attention when she was taught how to balance a budget. On marrying into the Delano clan of Roosevelts, she marveled at how they could be "generous in big things, because so little was ever wasted or spent in inconsequential ways."[1]

While her husband was governor of New York, she found paid work as an author and teacher. Later, as First Lady in the White House, she was criticized for continuing to earn money. The newspaper columnist Westbrook Pegler, in particular, claimed ER was using the position of First Lady to enrich herself.

ER found personal satisfaction in earning and spending her own money. She paid personal expenses, helped family members, and made substantial donations to charity. After FDR died, she declined the five-thousand-dollar pension awarded by Congress to the widows of previous presidents.

On Money and Finances

The best made budget is the one which used at most only seventy-five percent of a person's income, leaving a quarter to accumulate we hope, but in any case to be on hand to meet those very emergencies which are never expected but which always arise.[2]

August 15, 1936, "My Day"

[I]t is a great deal better for a husband and a wife to enter into an agreement before marriage as to how the family income shall be distributed, and it is well to have a distinct understanding of what part belongs to the wife and is hers exclusively.[3]

Circa 1946, *If You Ask Me*

I used to think that, of necessity, comfort and beauty cost a great deal of money. I have learned that that is not true. But I still think we encumber our lives with too much, and that perhaps that is the part of Gandhi's teaching that should remain with us today.[4]

January 27, 1953, "My Day"

It is pointless to discuss what is "enough" money. No two people would be likely to agree on what is "enough."[5]

Circa 1960, *You Learn by Living*

On Economics

There is absolutely no use in producing anything if you gradually reduce the number of people able to buy even the cheapest products. The only way to preserve our markets is to pay an adequate wage.[6]

March 1933, *Scribner's Magazine*

Even to dream, one must have a basis of economic security, and the dream is worth little if it can not provide that. Devotion to democracy, devotion to liberty, what we call patriotism, depends upon the realization of such conditions in our country as really give us the opportunity and hope for future dreams.[7]

January 6, 1941, "My Day"

[P]rices which go up must eventually come down, and the coming down process is a very difficult one.[8]

October 7, 1941, "My Day"

The kind of economy which is undertaken because of a vague feeling of fear about the future, is bad psychology for us all.[9]

November 7, 1941, "My Day"

All of the economic theories in the world translate themselves eventually to what happens to people in communities.[10]

January 9, 1942, "My Day"

It is enlightened selfishness to build up the ability of other nations to a higher standard of living. We thus produce wider markets for ourselves as well as the rest of the world.[11]

July 17, 1942, "My Day"

A subsidy is paid for by all the people, but in the end it costs us far less than runaway prices, which pile up indefinitely and cause a state of inflation.[12]

November 17, 1943, "My Day"

The economic situation cannot be left entirely in the hands of the industrialists themselves. It must have at least some supervision from government.[13]

July 19, 1944, "My Day"

Depression will be avoided if our financial and economic powers in our countries can understand that greed cannot be the motivating force.[14]

January 9, 1948, *New York Times*

It seems to me that one should sell to more people or develop markets in other countries, but that to oversell your own home market is apt to lose customers for you in the long run.[15]

February 15, 1949, "My Day"

On Wealth and Prosperity

Real prosperity can only come out when everybody prospers.[16]

March 19, 1936, "My Day"

The custom which existed for a time in this country, of having large places which cost a great deal of money and produced nothing beyond what one family used on their table, has always seemed to me a very wasteful tradition, and I am glad that it is rapidly disappearing.[17]

August 1, 1945, "My Day"

On Poverty

The question has never been decided whether a human being acquires more characteristics through heredity or through environment. Nevertheless I am quite sure that human beings who live in the Washington slums are conditioned to a great extent by their environment.[18]

April 22, 1949, "My Day"

Poverty is an expensive luxury. We cannot afford it.[19]

Circa 1963, *Tomorrow Is Now*

[P]overty is like a giant infection which contaminates every-thing—we know that unless we can eradicate it by the use of all our new scientific and economic materials, it can in time destroy us.[20]

Circa 1963, *Tomorrow Is Now*

On Capitalism

I'm not really very much interested in capitalism. I'm enormously interested in freedom and retaining the right to have whatever economy we want and to shape it as we want and having sufficient democracy so that the people actually hold their government in their own hands.[21]

November 23, 1957, interview by Mike Wallace

I'm a practical capitalist, I'm sure. But if we want to keep capi-talism, we in this country have got to learn that there must be real sharing, a real understanding, between management and labor. They must plan together because their interests are really identical.[22]

April 1, 1950, address to the Americans for Democratic Action

On the Stock Market

Does any one else get the impression, I wonder, from reading the newspapers . . . that there is little rhyme or reason to the going up or coming down of the Market?[23]

February 20, 1936, "My Day"

Eleanor Roosevelt autographing her book in Kansas City, Missouri, April 8, 1954.
Courtesy of the Franklin D. Roosevelt Library and Museum.

8 ✳ On Arts, Literature, and Leisure

Eleanor Roosevelt believed arts and literature were vital to the American nation. In her syndicated "My Day" newspaper column, she remarked on favorite authors like Steinbeck, Thackeray, Dickens, and Shakespeare.[1] She also shared details of her frequent visits to the theater, museums, and the ballet. During the Great Depression, she promoted struggling artists by ensuring that New Deal programs included work for unemployed professional actors, artists, musicians, and writers.[2]

Despite her privileged background, ER's columns, articles, and books were written for the average American. She might have quoted Spinoza, Don Quixote, and Kierkegaard,[3] but her advice and observations were down-to-earth and accessible.

Eleanor Roosevelt performing the "Eleanor Glide" at a square dance in Arthurdale, Virginia, May 27, 1938. Courtesy of the Franklin D. Roosevelt Library and Museum.

On Art and Artists

That is the great power of the artist, the power to make people hear and understand, through music, literature, or to paint something which we ordinary people feel but cannot reveal.[4]

September 1934, *American Magazine of Art*

All young civilizations are slow to recognize the value of their artists.[5]

Circa 1946, *If You Ask Me*

Photographs and movies will never be quite the same as paintings done by men who have lived with their subjects, who have seen the country and who know at first hand how the men working and fighting there actually feel.[6]

October 17, 1944, "My Day," on artists on the war front

We need not be artists, but we should be able to appreciate the work of artists.[7]

November 5, 1958, "My Day"

On Reading and Literature

I have no patience with people who try to give children books which they consider suitable to the youthful mind.[8]

July 25, 1932, *Time* magazine

Autobiographies are . . . only useful as the lives you read about and analyze may suggest to you something that you may find useful in your own journey through life.[9]

Circa 1937, *This Is My Story*

The reason that fiction is more interesting than any other form of literature to those of us who like to study people is that in fiction the author can really tell the truth without hurting anyone and without humiliating himself too much.[10]

Circa 1937, *This Is My Story*

But, after all, the value of anything which is written lies largely in its challenge to further thought and study.[11]

April 8, 1941, "My Day"

I think poetry read aloud is one of the great pleasures which companionable people may enjoy together.[12]

July 6, 1945, "My Day"

A love of good literature cannot be acquired just in school. It must be a part of the daily life of children in the home.[13]

November 15, 1954, "My Day"

What counts, in the long run, is not what you read. . . . It is the ideas stirred in your own mind, the ideas which are a reflection of your own thinking, which make you an interesting person.[14]

Circa 1960, *You Learn by Living*

It is often possible to gain more real insight into human beings and their motivations by reading great fiction than by personal acquaintance.[15]

Circa 1963, *Tomorrow Is Now*

No amount of TV watching will give you the satisfaction that comes from being able to read and re-read a book you have enjoyed.[16]

April 17, 1961, "My Day"

The reading of books should be a constant voyage of exploration, of adventure, of excitement. The habit of reading is a man's bulwark against loneliness, his window of opening on life, his unending delight. It is also an open door onto all the paths of knowledge and experience and beauty.[17]

Circa 1963, *Tomorrow Is Now*

On Writing

All writing and opinion is only good when you make it your own.[18]

June 15, 1933, White House press conference

So my plea is that those who have the gift of words, use them in these days to give the people hope by which to live and dream, for without the vision we shall perish.[19]

July 23, 1943, "My Day," exhortation during World War II

Writing is an art, and like all arts it constantly dangles before you the chance to do better, and so you can never be bored.[20]

March 4, 1944, "My Day"

On Theater, Film, and Television

"Great Theater" is undoubtedly the expression of the heart and mind of the people. Playwrights and actors are interpreters of the thought and feeling of their time.[21]

May 21, 1936, "My Day"

The film industry is a great industry, with infinite possibilities for good and bad. Its primary purpose is to entertain people. On the side, it can do many other things. It can popularize certain ideals, it can make education palatable. But in the long run, the judge who decides whether what it does is good or bad is the man or woman who attends the movies.[22]

October 29, 1947, "My Day," reaction to the Un-American Activities Committee's investigation of the film industry

Eleanor Roosevelt visiting a camp for Jewish émigrés to Israel in Campous, France, March 13, 1955. Courtesy of the Franklin D. Roosevelt Library and Museum.

9 ✳ On Education and Learning

Eleanor Roosevelt's early education occurred at home and was overseen by governesses. At fifteen, she journeyed to England to attend a French-language boarding school outside London called Allenswood. She later described her three years there as "the happiest of my life."[1]

Headmistress Marie Souvestre, a feminist liberal intellectual, took a special interest in the shy Roosevelt, encouraging and challenging her to think beyond her own experiences. With her guidance, ER grew more confident, excelled academically, and made friends. She also became one of her headmistress's favorite students.

As an adult, ER tried to pass on the lessons she learned at Allenswood to the next generation. In 1927, she and friends Marion Dickerman and Nancy Cook purchased Todhunter, a primary and secondary girls' school in New York City. ER taught courses in American history, English, American literature, and current events as part of the institution's mission to combine progressive and traditional education. ER found teaching very personally fulfilling, remarking, "I like it better than anything else I do."[2] ER reluctantly resigned after FDR was elected president because it became clear that she could not be both a teacher and First Lady. Although she never again taught in a classroom, ER educated wider audiences through her columns, articles, books, lectures, and radio interviews.

[E]ducation only ends with death.[3]

Circa 1928–30

[T]he point of real education is an ability to recognize the spirit that is in a real human being, even though it may be obscured for a time by lack of education or opportunity to observe social customs.[4]

October 1930, *Women's Journal*

I believe that education in government is one of the most important subjects for young people today.[5]

October 11, 1931, *New York Times*

The most important thing for a child is to acquire an attitude of responsibility. School is his job, and he should consider it as such.[6]

December 4, 1932, *New York Times Magazine*

The main thing in education, I have always thought, is the interest aroused in a young mind by stimulating, vivid personality.[7]

December 4, 1932, *New York Times*

We must equalize educational opportunities throughout the country. We must see that rural children have as good a general education as city children can acquire, and the advantages of both groups must if possible be made interchangeable. No city child should grow up without knowing the beauty of spring in the country or where milk comes from, how vegetables grow and what it is like to play in a field instead of on a city street. No country child who knows these things should be deprived, however, of museums, books, music and better teachers because it is easier to find them and to pay them in big cities than it is in rural districts.[8]

September 1936, *Parent's Magazine*

I think that we make a very serious mistake in education when we are terrified the minute anything is mentioned that we think might be a dangerous doctrine. It would be much better for youth to discuss any question in the world today with older people so that they can have two points of view.[9]

October 19, 1937, *New York Times*

Education comes to all of us through contact with things of beauty, wherever they may be. As we develop appreciation and understanding of new forms of beauty, we become rounded and educated human beings.[10]

March 19, 1941, "My Day"

It takes a good home and a good school to prepare young people for citizenship in a democracy and even then they will have to go on learning throughout life.[11]

Circa 1946, *If You Ask Me*

There should be a balance, I think, in education. We should never ignore the value of teaching every child how to use his hands, but at the same time a child should not be allowed to do that to a complete exclusion of the training of the mind.[12]

Circa 1941, *If You Ask Me*

Our interpretation of education must never be so narrow that we lose sight of the fact that learning to read on an empty stomach, or with eyes that are overstrained because of lack of proper eyeglasses, is not real education.[13]

January 12, 1942, "My Day"

[T]he best training in the world is practical experience.[14]

April 20, 1942, "My Day"

The importance of all education lies far more in the training of minds than in any facts which may be absorbed, for trained minds will ascertain the facts as they need to know them.[15]

December 30, 1942, "My Day"

If we look at education not as something to end at any special point, but as a preparation whereby we can attain the means to acquire whatever we need in life, we shall have a truer perspective on what we want to achieve through our educational system.[16]

December 30, 1942, "My Day"

Learning about other people does not mean that, of necessity, one must emulate them. It does mean one will have a better understanding of their motives and reactions and, therefore, will be a better neighbor.[17]

February 11, 1943, "My Day"

One of the best ways of enslaving a people is to keep them from education and thus make it impossible for them to understand what is going on in the world as a whole.[18]

May 11, 1943, "My Day"

The school houses of a community are not only for the use of the children and the educators. They should be the centers from which radiate the ideas which motivate the community.[19]

January 24, 1944, "My Day"

In a democracy such as ours, the education of all the people is a vital necessity. They cannot become articulate and express their beliefs unless they can both write and speak.[20]

November 3, 1945, "My Day"

[A]ll of life is a constant education.[21]

December 22, 1945, "My Day"

I think no matter how children learn to read, the stress should be on acquiring the habit of reading.[22]

Circa 1946, *If You Ask Me*

Nothing we learn in this world is ever wasted and I have come to the conclusion that practically nothing we do ever stands by itself. If it is good, it will serve some good purpose in the future. If it is evil, it may haunt us and handicap our efforts in unimagined ways.[23]

Circa 1949, *This I Remember*

We cannot afford to waste brains in this country. They are becoming more important to us every day. And surely financial position should not bar young people from the education which can give them positions of leadership in our nation in the future.[24]

February 22, 1951, "My Day"

Learning and living. But they are really the same thing, aren't they? There is no experience from which you can't learn something. When you stop learning you stop living in any vital and meaningful sense.[25]

Circa 1960, *You Learn by Living*

[I]f you are interested, you never have to look for new interests. They come to you. . . . All you need to do is to be curious, receptive, eager for experience.[26]

Circa 1960, *You Learn by Living*

And nothing you learn, however wide of the mark it may appear at the time, however trivial[,] is wasted.[27]

Circa 1960, *You Learn by Living*

You must be interested in anything that comes your way.[28] [italics in original]

Circa 1960, *You Learn by Living*

I am convinced that every effort must be made in childhood to teach the young to use their own minds. For one thing is sure: If they don't make up their minds, someone will do it for them.[29]

Circa 1960, *You Learn by Living*

What is essential is to train the mind so that it is capable of finding facts as it needs them, train it to learn how to learn.[30]

Circa 1960, *You Learn by Living*

What I have learned from my own experience is that the most important ingredients in a child's education are curiosity, interest, imagination, and a sense of adventure in life. You will find no courses in which these are taught.[31]

Circa 1960, *You Learn by Living*

Each new bit of knowledge, each new experience is an extra tool in meeting new problems and working them out.[32]

Circa 1960, *You Learn by Living*

In all my life, nothing I have ever learned has failed to be useful to me at some time or other, often in the most unexpected way and in some quite unforeseen context.[33]

Circa 1960, *You Learn by Living*

There is no human being from whom we cannot learn something if we are interested enough to dig deep.[34]

Circa 1960, *You Learn by Living*

None of us can afford to stop learning or to check our curiosity about new things, or to lose our humility in the face of new situations.[35]

Circa 1960, *You Learn by Living*

The average home in this country will buy a TV set before it will see to it that the children have the necessary books to read at home which will enrich their school courses.[36]

April 17, 1961, "My Day"

What we must learn to do is to create unbreakable bonds between the sciences and the humanities.[37]

Circa 1963, *Tomorrow Is Now*

On Education for Girls and Women

It has always been accepted as a truism that boys should be encouraged to be independent and take initiative. I think it is equally important in the education of a girl.[38]

December 1931, *Pictorial Review*

I do not feel that any girl should stay in college, who is not doing the maximum of work. I do not feel that, in these important years, girls should be chosen for college purely on the basis of whether they can afford to pay for this opportunity.[39]

December 17, 1942, "My Day"

On Teachers

I like to make the point that scholars and teachers are two very different things and that in the institutions which we call institutions of higher learning it seems to me we sometimes forget to give sufficient attention to the role of the teacher.[40]

February 8, 1936, "My Day"

We need better trained teachers, better paid teachers, teachers who can take a more active part in community life and who are given complete freedom in the expression of their opinions.[41]

April 19, 1943, "My Day"

Since we decided long ago that democracy could not exist without education, we can easily see why good teachers are essential to our development.[42]

January 24, 1944, "My Day"

We in the United States, I believe, sometimes lay too much stress on beautiful school buildings and not enough on compensating our teachers, without whom the buildings would be useless.[43]

May 21, 1957, "My Day"

On Knowledge

[I]ntellectual maturity requires a recognition of the fact that the world is full of things which no one human being can possibly know all about. The intellectually mature are usually anxious to learn and they know that not all wisdom is attained through winning university degrees.[44]

Circa 1946, *If You Ask Me*

We must join in an effort to use all knowledge for the good of all human beings. When we do that we shall have nothing to fear.[45]

Circa 1958, *On My Own*

Eleanor Roosevelt with Girl Scouts of Lexington, Kentucky, 1934. Courtesy of the Franklin D. Roosevelt Library and Museum.

10 ✺ On Gender, Age, and Class

As a young woman, the shy Eleanor Roosevelt seemed an unlikely crusader for women's rights. Her husband supported women's suffrage before she did.[1] But she also had strong female role models including her aunt Edith Livingston Hall and her feminist teacher Marie Souvestre.

ER joined a number of Progressive organizations that advocated for political, social, and economic reform. Among them were the Rivington Street Settlement House (1903–5), National Consumers League (1903–61), League of Women Voters (1920–28), Women's Division of the New York State Democratic Committee (1922–35), and the Women's Trade Union League (1922–55). Though she opposed the Equal Rights Amendment because she feared women would lose some of the protections gained in industry, she advocated for women's empowerment as part of the Progressive agenda. Later, under President Kennedy, she chaired the Commission on the Status of Women.

ER believed in the inherent equality of human beings regardless of race (see chapter 11), gender, class, or age. She showed concern for men and women from all walks of life, extending the same earnest interest and respect to a miner in West Virginia as she did to the queen of the Netherlands.

ER had an unshakable confidence that young people would make the world a better place and encouraged them to express themselves, even if they disagreed with her. When the American Youth Congress criticized the New Deal, she convinced the organization's leaders to help the administration shape Depression-era policies.

On Gender

There is no difference as between men and women, their duty being the same, to do the best they can.[2]

March 6, 1933, White House press conference

It is the person and not the sex which counts.[3]

Circa 1946, *If You Ask Me*

On Women

It may seem strange but no matter how plain a woman may be[,] if truth and loyalty are stamped upon her face all will be attracted to her & she will do good to all who come near her & those who know her well will always love her for they will feel her loyal spirit & have confidence in her.[4]

Circa 1899, when she was fifteen years old

No woman can really reach a place of recognition unless she has actually earned that place.[5]

July 9, 1934, radio broadcast at Simmons College

The thing I wanted to take you to task for is that phrase "she has the mind of a man." Why can't a woman think, be practical & a good business woman & still have a mind of her own?[6]

May 30, 1934, letter to Lorena Hickok

They say that women cannot laugh at themselves as men do. . . . Women find it difficult to get away from the habit of a lifetime which requires that they smooth out things for others, and oil the wheels of existence as they go their daily rounds, or perhaps we have a subtler way of expressing our humor.[7]

Circa December 1936

Our climate has some of the attributes of woman—it keeps us interested because it changes frequently![8]

August 7, 1936, "My Day"

When people say woman's place is in the home, I say, with enthusiasm, it certainly is, but if she really cares about her home, that caring will take her far and wide.[9]

August 25, 1935, *Saturday Evening Post*

When a woman fails, it is much more serious than when a man fails, because the average person attributes the failure not to the individual, but to the fact that she is a woman.[10]

March 1940, *Good Housekeeping*

It is perfectly obvious that women are not all alike. They do not think alike, nor do they feel alike on many subjects. Therefore, you can no more unite all women on a great variety of subjects than you can unite all men.[11]

April 1940, *Good Housekeeping*

It will always take all kinds of women to make up a world, and only now and then will they unite their interests. When they do, I think it is safe to say that something historically important will happen.[12]

April 1940, *Good Housekeeping*

There was a time when a woman married and her property became her husband's, her earnings were her husband's and the control of the children was never in her hands. The battle for the individual rights of women is one of long standing and none of us should countenance anything which undermines it.[13]

August 7, 1941, "My Day"

Women who want to lead must stand up and be shot at. More and more they are going to do it, and more and more they should do it.[14]

September 11, 1943, *Australian Women's Weekly*

When we look back over the achievements of women in the past and realize what handicaps they worked under, and think how very free we are today, it should give us a sense of confidence in our own possible achievements. Merely think of the dresses these women wore—then let's rejoice in our own ability to move freely, and let's go out and work harder.[15]

August 25, 1945, "My Day"

Women find themselves, in many cases, a minority group and are isolated in just the way that certain nationality and religious groups are.[16]

October 9, 1945, "My Day"

A woman will always have to be better than a man in any job she undertakes.[17]

November 29, 1945, "My Day"

So—against the odds the women inch forward, but I'm rather old to be carrying on the fight.[18]

February 13, 1946, letter to Joseph P. Lash

A woman cannot meet adequately the needs of those who are nearest to her if she has no interests, no friends, no occupations of her own.[19]

Circa 1960, *You Learn by Living*

Women have one advantage over men. Throughout history they have been forced to make adjustments. The result is that, in most cases, it is less difficult for a woman to adapt to new situations than it is for a man.[20]

Circa 1960, *You Learn by Living*

On Feminism

[I] took it for granted that men were superior creatures and knew more about politics than women did. I realized that if my husband was a suffragist I probably must be too [but] I cannot claim to have been a feminist in those early years.[21]

Circa 1937, *This Is My Story*

There is a great consciousness of feminism only when there are many wrongs to be righted.[22]

December 17, 1944, White House press conference

Every now and then I am reminded that even though the need for being a feminist is gradually disappearing in this country, we haven't quite reached the millennium.[23]

February 23, 1945, "My Day"

On the Equal Rights Amendment

[I]f we work to remove from our statute books those laws which discriminate against women today, we might accomplish more and do it in a shorter time than will be possible through the passage of this amendment.[24]

May 14, 1945, "My Day"

On Women in Politics

The whole point in women's suffrage is that the Government needs the point of view of all its citizens and women have a point of view which is of value to the Government.[25]

April 15, 1924, *New York Times*

The best education women can get is through talking politics in the home, through learning to play the game as men play it.[26]

April 20, 1924, *New York Times*

American women are backward about taking a serious and active part in politics. They have the vote, they have the power, but they don't seem to know what to do with it.[27]

April 20, 1924, *New York Times*

My message to women would be: "Get into the game and stay in it." Throwing mud from the outside won't help. Building up from the inside will.[28]

April 20, 1924, *New York Times*

[W]hile women now have the vote, they have not received serious consideration from the men leaders. There are virtually no women who have any actual influence or say in things that really count, in either party.[29]

April 8, 1928, *New York Times*

Men who work hard in party politics are always recognized, or taken care of in one way or another. Women, most of whom are voluntary workers and not at all self-seeking, are generally expected to find in their labor its own reward. When it comes to giving the offices or dealing out favors, men are always given precedence.[30]

April 1928, *Red Book Magazine*

Where victory is certain, very rarely can you get a woman nominated on the party ticket.[31]

April 1928, *Red Book Magazine*

If women believe they have a right and duty in political life today, they must learn to talk the language of men. They must not only master the phraseology, but also understand the machinery which men have built up through years of practical experience. Against the men bosses there must be women bosses who can talk as equals, with the backing of a coherent organization of women voters behind them.[32]

April 1928, *Red Book Magazine*

[It is] impossible for husband and wife both to have political careers. . . . It requires all the energy and united effort of an entire household to support one.[33]

October 1932, *Liberty*

Certainly, a woman can be elected President—in all probability, sometime a women will be—but she *may* not, in my opinion be elected at the present time or in the near future.[34]

October 1935, *Cosmopolitan*

[W]omen are tired when they come home at night and certainly it requires effort to go out to hear a political speaker! You may be amused now and then but you are often bored. Nevertheless your vote is a matter of real importance.[35]

February 3, 1936, "My Day"

[A]ll women in public life needed to develop skin as tough as rhinoceros hide.[36]

Circa 1936

[W]omen as a whole do not back women's running and do not back them for positions and are not really trying to get them to represent the woman's point of view. . . . [A]s soon as you have found a genuine demand among women for the representation of their point of view, you will find plenty of women capable and willing to run.[37]

December 27, 1938, White House press conference

No revolution has come about because women have been given the vote.[38]

March 1940, *Good Housekeeping*

Women have had suffrage now for so many years, that it is easy to forget what we owe to the women who fought for our enfranchisement, who persuaded and cajoled and browbeat the gentlemen who held our destinies in their hands.[39]

May 19, 1941, "My Day," regarding Carrie Chapman Catt

I hope the women of the United States will awaken to the full sense of the influence which they can wield if they accept the responsibility which all power implies.[40]

December 10, 1942, "My Day"

Women with their understanding of human living problems, lie at the basis of the kind of citizenship that will be developed after the war. They can determine whether there remains peace in the future; whether the people have better opportunities and whether there is to be a solid foundation for world progress.[41]

October 21, 1943, *Western Mail* (Perth, Australia)

Men and women both are not yet enough accustomed to following a woman and looking to her for leadership.[42]

July 9, 1946, *Look*

If, however, it is possible for a woman to run for office and fill whatever other obligations she has, I think that is a part of her obligation as a citizen, just as it is with men.[43]

Circa 1946, *If You Ask Me*

On Men

Men tend to look at things from a legalistic point of view; women from a practical one.[44]

October 1932, *Liberty*

[A]s a rule women know not only what men know, but much that men will never know. For, how many men really know the heart and soul of a woman?[45]

March 6, 1937, "My Day"

Men do not instinctively revolt against war as women do.[46]

Circa 1949, *This I Remember*

Mine was another day spent wondering what men do in their businesses, they are so slow on committees![47]

June 30, 1940, letter to Lorena Hickok

I have always thought that this desire to prove yourself on equal terms with your fellow men, exists very strongly in men who have never had an opportunity to mix with a great variety of men and, therefore, are a little uncertain of themselves.[48]

August 21, 1943, "My Day"

It seems hard for men to understand that any decent woman doesn't just love a man's "outside." It is what he is in mind & heart & soul that matters.[49]

April 27, 1944, letter to Joseph P. Lash

You males are so conceited! Women don't need masculine intelligence, female brains can work along with you & often give you a helping hand.[50]

June 3, 1944, letter to Joseph P. Lash

It is said that gossip is the vice of women. Yet I have lived nearly sixty years, during which I have spent a good part of my time with men, and I have not found that they are any less quick to repeat things about which they know little.[51]

September 25, 1944, "My Day"

[M]en of honest convictions, though they may differ, are bound to make a contribution to the thinking of the world.[52]

October 12, 1944, "My Day," on the death of Wendell Willkie, her husband's opponent in the 1940 presidential campaign

I find that, if anything, the men here take more words to express their thoughts than women. The answer will doubtless be that they have more thoughts to express . . . but if you want to get work done quickly[,] oratory is not half as important as putting your thoughts clearly.[53]

February 13, 1946, "My Day"

Almost always the male animal is the showoff while the female remains demure and is less startlingly clad. Perhaps someday we will have the courage to strike a good medium and let the men have a little self-expression in their clothes.[54]

July 13, 1951, "My Day"

On Men in Politics

The machinery of party politics has always been in the hands of men, and still is. Our statesmen and legislators are still keeping in form as the successors of the early warriors gathering around the campfire plotting the next day's attack.[55]

April 1928, *Red Book Magazine*

Beneath the veneer of courtesy and outward show of consideration universally accorded women, there is a widespread male hostility—age-old, perhaps—against sharing with them any actual control.[56]

April 1928, *Red Book Magazine*

The men can't do that. They just don't have the imagination.[57]

November 4, 1943, *New York Times,* on men representing women in politics

On Children

They naturally desire to know about the world in which they live, and if they lose that curiosity, it is usually because we grown people are so stupid.[58]

August 24, 1935, *Saturday Evening Post*

Every child in a family is a link with the future. . . . It makes one want to live to see the future and at the same time it is the kind of hostage which makes one more willing to lay down one's arms![59]

July 16, 1936, "My Day"

But all children, it seems to me, have a right to food, shelter, and equal opportunity for education and an equal chance to come into the world healthy and get the care they need through their early years to keep them well and happy.[60]

June 15, 1940, *Collier's*

What happens to our children is the concern of the whole nation because a democracy requires a standard of citizenship which no other form of government finds necessary.[61]

June 15, 1940, *Collier's*

We are concerned about the children before they are born, but we should follow them through every step of their development until the children are firmly on their feet and started in life as citizens of a democracy.[62]

June 15, 1940, *Collier's*

As long as we have babies we renew our sense of security that the world we know is going to survive.[63]

June 26, 1943, "My Day"

On Youth

In the hands of the young people lies the future of this country, perhaps the future of the world and our civilization. They need what help they can get from the older generation and yet it must be sympathetically given with a knowledge that in the last analysis the young people themselves must make their own decisions.[64]

August 1933, *Woman's Home Companion*

I have moments of real terror when I think we may be losing this generation. We have got to bring these young people into the active life of the community and make them feel that they are necessary.[65]

Circa May 1934

As long as you can get fun out of life, even if you are near the starvation point, youth and hope will win out I am sure. When the rest of us are trying to play safe and think of the wise things to do, these young things will enjoy life and probably get a lot more out of it than any of us who are old and sensible.[66]

February 18, 1936, "My Day"

Youth should not be pampered, but they should be treated fairly and sympathetically. They must learn by their own mistakes, but we must not make them feel that their mistakes are irretrievable.[67]

April 20, 1940, *Liberty*

I always feel that it is a great responsibility and a tremendous challenge to talk to youth, because anything less than complete sincerity is detected and discounted.[68]

September 4, 1942, "My Day"

I am afraid I am just incurably fond of being with young people.[69]

December 14, 1942, "My Day"

Young people have a disconcerting way of asking direct questions about subjects their elders would be somewhat reluctant to bring out in the open.[70]

October 5, 1945, "My Day"

It is always a rather solemn thing to face rows and rows of young people and realize that the world opening up for them is a strange and difficult one for which neither their elders nor frequently their schools have been able to prepare them very well. It is also a heartening thing, however, to see them rise to the challenges that are put up to them.[71]

June 29, 1951, "My Day"

On Aging and the Responsibilities of Being an Elder

It's good to be middle-aged. Things don't matter so much. You don't take it so hard when things happen to you that you don't like.[72]

October 11, 1932, on her forty-eighth birthday

I have a theory that when you get to be my age, birthdays shouldn't be a time to celebrate. The more you forget your birthdays as you grow older, the younger you stay.[73]

October 11, 1934, *New York Times*

[A]s we grow older we tend more to compromise. That is why I believe we should always have youth and age together when decisions of importance are made in government circles. The two points of view are needed to balance the scales and achieve wise decisions.[74]

April 3, 1942, "My Day"

I think, perhaps, the function of older people in times of stress like these, is to keep islands of quiet in themselves where youth may take refuge. I fail in this very badly at times.[75]

September 17, 1942, "My Day"

Really to serve well, age should free one from false values. It should make it easy to cling to the essentials and to make one more aware of the joys of life, because the time is shorter and there is more urgency to live abundantly.[76]

October 13, 1942, "My Day"

One always hopes that each year one gains added wisdom, but, at least, if one gains an increasing number of friends, there is a satisfaction in piled-up years.[77]

October 16, 1943, "My Day"

It is a pity that we can not have the experience that comes with age in our younger days, when we really need it. We certainly would enjoy life more and I am sure that somehow the responsibilities would all be taken care of quite as well.[78]

Circa 1949, *This I Remember*

A mature person is one who does not think only in absolutes, who is able to be objective even when deeply stirred emotionally, who has learned that there is both good and bad in all people and in all things, and who walks humbly and deals charitably with the circumstances of life, knowing that in this world no one is all-knowing and therefore all of us need both love and charity.[79]

October 1953, *McCall's Magazine*

Old people love their own things even more than young people do. It means so much to sit in the same old chair you sat in for a great many years, to see the same pictures that you always looked at! [80]

Circa February 1934

The greatest contribution the older generation can give, I think, to the younger generation, is the feeling that there is someone to fall back upon, more especially when the hard times come up upon them. This is so even when we know that we have brought those hard times upon ourselves.[81]

November 9, 1938, "My Day"

Many people are as vigorous at sixty-five as they were at forty-five, with the added advantage of years of experience. Yet they often face compulsory retirement. If such people are wise they may arrange to go somewhere else, where their past experience is appreciated and where they can exercise the same profession.[82]

Circa 1960, *You Learn by Living*

So it is a major part of maturity to accept not only your own short-comings but those of the people you love, and help them not to fail when you can.[83]

Circa 1960, *You Learn by Living*

The greatest tragedy of old age is the tendency for the old to feel unneeded, unwanted, and of no use to anyone; the secret to happiness in the declining years is to remain interested in life, as active as possible, useful to others, busy, and forward looking.[84]

Circa 1962, *Eleanor Roosevelt's Book of Common Sense Etiquette*

On Class

Children coming from a home where there is just money enough to give them healthful surroundings but where they are obliged to struggle to a certain extent to obtain opportunities for progress have an advantage over children who always have dropped into their laps the greatest of opportunities for development with no effect on their own part.[85]

June 1931, *Parent's Magazine*

It always amuses me when any group of people take it for granted that because they have been privileged for a generation or two they are set apart in any way from the man or woman who is working in order to keep the wolf from the door. It is only luck and a little veneer, temporarily on the surface, and before very long the wheels may turn and one and all must fall back on whatever basic "quality" they have.[86]

Circa 1937, *This Is My Story*

I find royalty heavy & boring.[87]

September 6, 1940, letter to Lorena Hickok

Royalty is a strain even when it is simple & stodgy.[88]

June 24, 1943, letter to Joseph P. Lash

The only difference between Royalty and other guests is that Royalty takes up more space.[89]

September 11, 1943, *Australian Women's Weekly*

11 ☀ On Race and Ethnicity

As a young woman, Eleanor Roosevelt shared the prejudices common among her class. She looked down upon immigrants, African Americans, and Jews.[1] Her opinions began to change when
she volunteered at a settlement house on New York's Lower East
Side. Later, as an investigator for New York's Consumers' League,

Eleanor Roosevelt and Marian Anderson, May 22, 1953. Courtesy of the Franklin D.
Roosevelt Library and Museum.

she inspected the miserable living and working conditions of tenements and sweatshops. These experiences transformed ER into a champion of minority rights.

Although she spoke out against injustice and promoted tolerance, it was her actions, often performed in her trademark matter-of-fact manner, which marked her as a woman before her time. As First Lady, she defied Washington, D.C.'s segregation laws by hosting African Americans at the White House. She publicly supported antilynching legislation, and in 1939 ER resigned from the Daughters of the American Revolution when the group refused to allow Marian Anderson to sing at Constitution Hall. During World War II, when visiting the Tuskegee Airmen, she defied convention and her flummoxed security detail to fly with the African American pilots.

Such activism caused friction, especially in the South. ER faced bomb threats and even death threats. In 1958, the Ku Klux Klan offered a twenty-five-thousand-dollar reward for kidnapping her.[2]

During the 1930s, ER became alarmed at European anti-Semitism. She urged FDR to support the 1939 Wagner-Rogers Bill, an unsuccessful attempt to admit twenty thousand Jewish child refugees into the country. Though she opposed the creation of a Jewish state immediately after the war, her position later changed. ER visited Israel three times before her death.

On Tolerance

There is no reason why all the races in this country should not live together each of them giving from their particular gift something to the other, and contributing an example to the world of "peace on earth, good will toward men."[3]

August 24, 1935, *Saturday Evening Post*

We must be proud of every one of our citizens, for regardless of nationality, or race, every one contributes to the welfare and culture of the nation.[4]

November 1938, speech at the Southern Conference on Human Welfare

I think people should be allowed to do whatever they want to do as long as it doesn't interfere with the rights of any other individual and as long as it's the law and doesn't interfere with the rights of any other people.[5]

May 13, 1941, White House press conference

Real tolerance does not attempt to make other people conform to any particular religious or racial pattern. We are within our rights, of course, in refusing to go to church with another man if we do not like this church, but we are certainly not within our rights in condemning him because he attends that church.[6]

February 1940, *Cosmopolitan*

We cannot force people to accept friends for whom they have no liking, but living in a democracy it is entirely reasonable to demand that every citizen of that democracy enjoy the fundamental rights of a citizen.[7]

May 11, 1942, *New Republic*

I am afraid with a good many people tolerance is a matter of indifference. But, when it has its roots in the security of one's convictions and beliefs, then tolerance can be a very fine thing. In that kind of tolerance there is true humility which, in spite of personal conviction, listens and tries to understand other points of view.[8]

May 26, 1942, "My Day"

What is really important is not what religion or race we belong to, but how we live our lives.[9]

June 19, 1943, "My Day"

Tolerance ought only to be the preliminary step which allows us to get to know other people, and which prevents us from setting up bars, just because they may be of a different race or religion. The real value of any relationship is the fact that we learn to like people in spite of our differences.[10]

November 24, 1943, "My Day"

I do not like the word tolerance. If you tolerate something, you do not like it very much.[11]

July 1945, *Coronet*

As I grow older, it seems to me important that there be no greater stress laid on our divisions, but that we stress as much as possible our agreements.[12]

July 23, 1949, letter to Cardinal Spellman

It is not our job to change people's customs. It is our job to know what they are and, if possible, to understand them.[13]

Circa 1960, *You Learn by Living*

Certainly we must face the evidence that the color of the skin does not regulate the superiority or inferiority of the individual.[14]

Circa 1963, *Tomorrow Is Now*

On Intolerance

I do not believe that oppression anywhere or injustice which is tolerated by the people of any country toward any group in that country is a healthy influence. I feel that unless we learn to live together as individuals and as groups, and to find ways of settling our difficulties without showing fear of each other and resorting to force, we cannot hope to see our democracy successful.[15]

January 1939, *Virginia Quarterly Review*

There is a growing wave in this country of fear, and of intolerance which springs from fear. Sometimes it is a religious intolerance, sometimes it is a racial intolerance, but all intolerance grows from the same roots.[16]

January 1939, *Virginia Quarterly Review*

Perhaps the wave of anti-Semitism is our greatest manifestation of intolerance today, though in some places anti-Catholicism runs a close second, and in others fear of the Negro's aspirations is paramount.[17]

February 1940, *Cosmopolitan*

[E]nding unemployment will, to a very great extent, end intolerance.[18]

February 1940, *Cosmopolitan*

On Prejudice and Racism

We can have no group beaten down, underprivileged without reaction of the rest.[19]

May 11, 1934, NBC radio broadcast

To remain as a member implies approval of that action, and therefore I am resigning.[20]

February 27, 1939, "My Day," resignation from the Daughters of the American
Revolution following the group's refusal to allow Marian Anderson to sing at their hall

When we permit religious prejudice to gain headway in our midst, when we allow one group of people to look down upon another, then we may for a short time bring hardship on some particular group of people, but the real hardship and the real wrong is done to democracy and to our nation as a whole. We are then breeding people who cannot live under a democratic form of government but must be controlled by force.[21]

January 1939, *Virginia Quarterly Review*

[F]or the more we know about each other and about our contributions to the good things in our country, the less we shall be liable to fall a victim to that most pernicious thing called: "racial and religious prejudice."[22]

September 18, 1941, "My Day"

If we cannot meet the challenge of fairness to our citizens of every nationality, . . . if we cannot keep in check anti-Semitism, anti-racial feelings as well as anti-religious feelings, then we shall have removed from the world, the one real hope for the future on which all humanity must now rely.[23]

December 16, 1941, "My Day"

The psychology which believes that the white man alone of all the races in the world, has something which must be imposed on all other races, must go. We know today that our chance to live in peace in the future lies in respect for the individual, no matter what his color. We must have a willingness to accept what anyone has to contribute to civilization, and to cooperate in the difficult business of "live and let live."[24]

April 3, 1942, "My Day"

We must keep moving forward steadily, removing restrictions which have no sense, and fighting prejudice. If we are wise we will do this where it is easiest to do it first, and watch it spread gradually to places where the old prejudices are slow to disappear.[25]

May 11, 1942, *New Republic*

Courage belongs to no one race or no one religion. . . . [I]f any of us ever had any prejudices we can beat them down and hide them away, shamed by the mute testimony of the names on our casualty lists.[26]

May 19, 1943, "My Day," remark made during World War II

We never know where prejudices will lead us. Neither do we know how often we use our prejudices to excuse or cloak motives and emotions which we would be ashamed to bring into the light of day.[27]

December 16, 1944, "My Day"

[N]o racial prejudices are born in us. They are acquired as children live with adults who have prejudices, racial and religious.[28]

July 17, 1945, "My Day"

[I]f silence seems to give approval, then remaining silent is cowardly.[29]

Circa 1946, *If You Ask Me,* on speaking out against prejudice

The same God created all human beings and He certainly never intended that we should have less respect for any one of His creatures than for another.[30]

Circa 1946, *If You Ask Me*

[T]he Ku Klux Klan is just what it always has been—a secret, terroristic organization, hopeful of enforcing the warped ideas of a few hoodlums on a defenseless minority![31]

December 22, 1948, radio broadcast

Unless indoctrinated, a child is too logical to understand discrimination.[32]

Circa 1960, *You Learn by Living*

[P]rejudice so blinds us that we see only what we expect to see, what we want to see.[33]

Circa 1963, *Tomorrow Is Now*

On Native Americans

Now the Indians in our midst were the original owners of our country, and it seems ironical to me to practice discrimination against them.[34]

October 3, 1960, "My Day"

On Jews and Anti-Semitism

I'd rather be hung than seen at [a party that was] mostly Jews.[35]

January 22, 1918, letter to Sara Roosevelt

It is the secret fear that the Jewish people are stronger or more able than those who still wield superior physical power over them, which brings about oppression. I believe that those nations which do not persecute are saved only by confidence in themselves and a feeling that they can still defend themselves and their own place in the world. Therefore, I am forced to the conclusion that the Jewish people though they may be in part responsible for the present situation are not as responsible as the other races who need to examine themselves and grapple with their own fears.[36]

December 31, 1938, *Liberty*

The Jews are like all the other people of the world. There are able people among them, there are courageous people among them, there are people of extraordinary intellectual ability along many lines. There are people of extraordinary integrity and people of great beauty and great charm. On the other hand, largely because of environment and economic conditions, there are people among them who cringe, who are dishonest, who try to take advantage of their neighbors, who are aggressive and unattractive. In other words, they are a cross-section of the human race, just as is every other nationality and every other religious group.[37]

August 13, 1943, "My Day"

Jewish people themselves can help by trying to be as natural and unselfconscious as possible. They can go about their own lives, doing the things they have always done, but trying not to be too aggressive or too ingratiating or too flattering to the people who they suspect are sizing them up.[38]

Circa 1946, *If You Ask Me,* on how Jews could overcome anti-Semitism

As you go back into history you realize that persecution under which the Jews have suffered in country after country has made them the strong, resourceful, resilient people that they are today. They have almost always had to be more intelligent and work harder in order to cope with the restrictions placed on them.[39]

May 13, 1960, "My Day"

On African Americans

It seems trite to say to the Negro, you must have patience, when he has had patience so long; you must not expect miracles overnight, when he can look back to the years of slavery and say—how many nights! he has waited for justice.[40]

May 11, 1942, *New Republic*

I guess Negroes can fly.[41]

April 19, 1941, response to her flight with Tuskegee airman
Charles "Chief" Anderson

If I were a Negro today, I think I would have moments of great bitterness. It would be hard for me to sustain my faith in democracy and to build up a sense of goodwill toward men of other races.[42]

October 1943, *Negro Digest*

Music is distinctly a field in which the Negro people have a great gift.[43]

February 23, 1944, "My Day"

[T]hey should, by every peaceful means possible, push for their rights which are the heritage of every citizen in a democracy, but they have to be patient and try to avoid rioting and bloodshed.[44]

Circa 1946, *If You Ask Me*

I have no feeling that the colored race is inferior to the white race. Given the same opportunities over several generations, they have produced artists, scientists, educators and many valuable citizens. I would certainly have no objection if a child of mine chose a friend among the peoples of any race, regardless of color or creed.[45]

Circa 1946, *If You Ask Me*

Some of my best friends are negro.[46]

November 1975, *Ebony*

I value and enjoy my Negro friends equally with my white friends.[47]

November 1975, *Ebony*

Sometimes my Negro friends praise me because they think I have sacrificed too much for them. There have been no great sacrifices because all friendships are rewarding.[48]

November 1975, *Ebony*

The more whites and Negroes become friends and lose whatever self-consciousness they started out with, we shall have a much happier world.[49]

November 1975, *Ebony*

On Segregation

[M]any of the things which we deplore, the prevalence of tuberculosis, the mounting record of crime in certain sections of the country, are not due just to lack of education and to physical differences, but are due in great part to the basic fact of segregation which we have set up in this country and which warps and twists the lives not only of our Negro population, but sometimes of foreign born or even religious groups.[50]

November 11, 1941, letter

A major part of my criticism has been on the Negro question, of course, . . . and I think that it is quite natural because to some people it seems to be destroying something that to them is very dear.[51]

November 23, 1957, interview by Mike Wallace, referring to her efforts to counter segregation

On Racial Intermarriage

Some people have written me to ask me if I was advocating mixed marriage and I would like to make it clear that I would never advocate this. It seems to me that in the mixing of racial strains, the difficulties which always exist in any marriage are greatly enhanced. Races will mix however, even in this country, we see the evidences of this mixture.[52]

July 29, 1943, "My Day"

On Immigrants

[M]any a good citizen not born in this country has, perhaps, a greater appreciation of what it means to live in a free and self-governing country and, therefore, a greater sense of responsibility for preserving the democratic way of life.[53]

August 7, 1943, "My Day"

[W]e should never have allowed any group to settle as groups where they created little German or Japanese or Scandinavian "islands" and did not melt into our general pattern.[54]

October 16, 1943, *Collier's*

On Refugees

We, in this country, are opposing totalitarian government. We do not like Nazi or Fascist regimes. But we are not opposing the refugees who want to help us make our country safe, nor citizens who have come to us from other lands and who are loyal and good Americans. This demands from us a refusal to be hysterical and an ability to use our powers of observation, but to use them wisely.[55]

May 21, 1941, "My Day"

Prejudices and feelings must be put aside and the whole refugee problem looked upon as an economic one.[56]

Circa 1953, *India and the Awakening East*

The refugees of the world are a constant and a painful reminder of the breakdown of civilization through the stupidity of war.[57]

Circa 1961, *The Autobiography of Eleanor Roosevelt*

On Assimilation

Perhaps when a baby is born on our soil or when an individual becomes naturalized, he ought to be given the opportunity, if he desires it, to change his foreign name to its American equivalent. . . . What is wrong about changing Lowenstein to Livingston, Rabinowitz to Robinson, or any of these comparatively foreign names to simpler versions? . . . We should welcome and honor people willing to take this step toward Americanization. It may prove to be a most important factor in bringing about a more unified American people.[58]

July 14, 1945, *Liberty*

Eleanor Roosevelt, Lorena Hickok, and others in Puerto Rico, March 7, 1934. Courtesy of the Franklin D. Roosevelt Library and Museum.

12 ☀ On Humanity and Human Characteristics

Eleanor Roosevelt's opinions about human beings and their characteristics demonstrate her great respect and curiosity about people of all ages and from all walks of life. Despite a privileged upbringing that could have given her a sense of superiority, she considered all human beings equal and worthy of respect.

On Humanity

Human beings are poor things, think how much discipline we need ourselves & don't get too discouraged.[1]

January 29, 1934, letter to Lorena Hickok

The great experiences of life are the same wherever you live and whether you are rich or poor. Birth and death, courage and cowardice, kindness and cruelty, love and hate, are no respecters of persons, and they are the occasions and emotions which bring about most of the experience of life.[2]

August 24, 1935, *Saturday Evening Post*

Human beings either must recognize the fact that what serves the people as a whole serves them best as individuals, and through selfish or unselfish interests, they become people of good intentions and honesty.[3]

Circa 1938, "This Troubled World"

[H]uman beings are so mad, I believe, that they must always be conquering something, even if it is only their own indolence.[4]

Circa 1938, *My Days*

Without doubt human beings are the most interesting study in the world.[5]

January 5, 1939, "My Day"

We do not dwell upon man's lower nature any more than we have to in life, but we know it exists and we pass over it charitably and we are surprised how much there is of fineness that comes out of the baser clay.[6]

June 28, 1939, "My Day"

If human beings can be trained for cruelty and greed and a belief in power which comes through hate and fear and forces, certainly we can train equally well for gentleness and mercy and the power of love which come because of the strength of the good qualities to be found in the soul of every individual human being.[7]

Circa 1940, "The Moral Basis of Democracy"

Human beings are about as unpredictable as the weather![8]

January 4, 1941, "My Day"

I find that the people who have the most difficult time in life are the perfectionists who never learn to get along as well as they can, but keep worrying because things are not as perfect as they should be.[9]

August 12, 1942, "My Day"

It is still the people who have the most self-control, who return the soft word, even when they feel they are in the right, who make the real contribution to a world in which peace may be possible in the future.[10]

December 13, 1943, "My Day"

[I]t is the sum total of what we do as individuals that makes the world.[11]

August 9, 1943, "My Day"

Even in our blackest moment, we have to acknowledge that there is something very fine in human beings.[12]

November 3, 1943, "My Day"

Queer when one evaluates human relationships how few go very deep.[13]

January 6, 1944, letter to Joseph P. Lash

We cannot hope to build faith in ourselves by being suspicious of other people. We need not be "suckers," but neither need we be exploiters.[14]

May 30, 1944, "My Day"

The more I observe human nature, the more I feel we are all of us perverse![15]

June 13, 1944, "My Day"

As a matter of fact most people want to be told, they don't want to decide for themselves. They like to be able to blame someone afterwards if they make a wrong decision![16]

July 20, 1944, letter to Joseph P. Lash

I could almost wish that God had not given weak human beings quite so much freedom, for we make of his beautiful world such a sorry place at times.[17]

August 19, 1944, "My Day"

When people's hearts are freed by sympathy and sorrow, it makes them wonderfully kind.[18]

April 18, 1945, "My Day," following the death of FDR

We may be taught by our church or our government, or our family, to hate certain elements of a society, but the love man has for his brother or for his wife and that both of them have for their children is a human, not a political value.[19]

Circa 1945

I doubt if any human beings, just by themselves, are very important; but when they start a new trend of thought and action, they are apt to symbolize for their contemporaries and for the future a new idea, and therefore become important.[20]

Circa 1946, If You Ask Me

It is wise, I think, to teach children that intrinsically every human being has the same value before his Maker.[21]

Circa 1946, If You Ask Me

I honor the human race. When it faces life head-on, it can almost remake itself.[22]

Circa 1960, You Learn by Living

[U]ntil one sees with one's own eyes and comes to feel with one's own heart, one will never understand other people.[23]

Circa 1960, You Learn by Living

If you approach each new person you meet in a spirit of adventure you will find that you become increasingly interested in them and endlessly fascinated by the new channels of thought and experience and personality that you encounter. I don't mean simply the famous people of the world, but the people from every walk and condition of life.[24]

Circa 1960, You Learn by Living

I think that one of the strangest qualities in every human being is the need to feel needed, to feel essential, to feel important. Too often our own youngsters do not feel that they are really essential to their country, or to the scheme of things.[25]

Circa 1961, *The Autobiography of Eleanor Roosevelt*

I think that one of the reasons it is so difficult for us, as a people, to understand other areas of the world is that we cannot put ourselves imaginatively in their place.[26]

Circa 1961, *The Autobiography of Eleanor Roosevelt*

The world cannot be understood from a single point of view.[27]

Circa 1963, *Tomorrow Is Now*

Human resources are the most valuable assets the world has.[28]

Circa 1963, *Tomorrow Is Now*

It is tragic to realize that the majority of human beings, even the so-called educated, call upon only the smallest fraction of their potential capacity.[29]

Circa 1963, *Tomorrow Is Now*

If we want a free and peaceful world, if we want to make the deserts bloom and man grow to greater dignity as a human being—WE CAN DO IT![30]

Circa 1963, *Tomorrow Is Now*

On Civilization

You and I may be hated by our neighbors, but if we know about it we try to change things within us which brought it about. That is the way civilized people develop. Murder and annihilation are never a satisfactory answer, for the few who escape grow up more bitter against their persecutors and a day of reckoning always comes.[31]

August 13, 1943, "My Day"

Some day, perhaps, the world will be the kind of civilized place in which we can all live safely according to our own likes. But it isn't that kind of place today.[32]

June 21, 1944, "My Day," comment made during World War II

If we desire our civilization to survive, then we must accept the responsibility of constructive work and of the wise use of knowledge greater than any ever achieved by man before.[33]

August 8, 1945, "My Day"

[T]he collective intelligence of mankind should be able to save the world from suicide, and yet nothing seems to indicate that such is the case. We follow the path of the years gone by and we feel a little of the inevitableness of the Greek tragedy.[34]

December 20, 1950, "My Day"

On Beauty

It should be a consolation to us plain people that a child's conception of beauty, as far as the people they love are concerned, has nothing whatsoever to do with perfect features or beautiful coloring. . . . Looks have little to do with their appreciation of the person.[35]

August 10, 1943, "My Day"

On Charm

[C]harm is the ability to forget oneself and be engrossed in other people.[36]

Circa 1946, *If You Ask Me*

On Conscience

When will our consciences grow so tender that we will act to prevent human misery rather than avenge it?[37]

February 16, 1946, "My Day," reaction to visiting the Zeilsheim Jewish displaced-persons camp

On Courage

Every time we shirk making up our minds or standing up for a cause in which we believe, we weaken our character and our ability to be fearless.[38]

January 1939, *Virginia Quaterly Review*

Courage is more exhilarating than fear and in the long run it is easier. We do not have to become heroes overnight. Just a step at a time, meeting each thing that comes up, seeing it is not as dreadful as it appeared, discovering we have the strength to stare it down.[39]

Circa 1960, *You Learn by Living*

We must know what we think and speak out, even at the risk of unpopularity.[40]

Circa 1963, *Tomorrow Is Now*

On Curiosity

Curiosity will prevent your being closed behind a barrier, and will add, day by day, to your imagination and make your contacts increasingly easy.[41]

August 24, 1935, *Saturday Evening Post*

It is not always our own fault when we lack curiosity, for our environment may have prevented its development. The lack of curiosity in parents will often mean that they will try to eliminate it in their younger children, and thus keep their homes from stimulating the youthful urge to acquire knowledge.[42]

August 24, 1935, *Saturday Evening Post*

You cannot prevent unhappiness or sorrow entering into any life—even the fairy godmother of legend could not give freedom from these experiences—but curiosity will ensure an ever-recurring interest in life and will give you the needed impetus to turn your most baleful experience to some kind of service.[43]

August 24, 1935, *Saturday Evening Post*

On Imagination

This power of imagination is a kind of defense in childhood. You get away from realities. It makes you important to yourself. If used correctly, it makes it more possible for you later on to imagine what other people are like and what they think and feel. It helps to keep you curious, anxious to understand what is going on around you.[44]

Circa 1960, *You Learn by Living*

On Kindness

[T]he basis of all good human behavior is kindness.[45]

Circa 1962, *Eleanor Roosevelt's Book of Common Sense Etiquette*

On Growth

People grow through experiences, if they meet life honestly and courageously. This is how character is built and young people recognize this ability to grow in those with whom they come in contact.[46]

August 2, 1941, "My Day"

Life is interesting only as long as it is a process of growth; or, to put it another way, we can grow only as long as we are interested.[47]

Circa 1960, *You Learn by Living*

On Honesty and Truth

[W]hen I'm sure something that is said is not true, it doesn't bother me at all. With experience you come to know that in the long run the truth will come out.[48]

October 10, 1954, *New York Times*

But the withholding of information from a child either frustrates him or makes him seek it for himself. And the trouble with the latter method is that it is apt to make the child feel both guilty and dishonest.[49]

Circa 1960, *You Learn by Living*

Until you have been able to face the truth about yourself you cannot be really sympathetic or understanding in regard to what happens to other people.[50]

Circa 1960, *You Learn by Living*

On Hospitality

In short being a good hostess is an art but an art which is built on tact and consideration for others, joined with the kind of efficiency which makes the wheels go round without too much obvious oiling.[51]

June 19, 1936, "My Day"

From long experience I have decided that the perfect hostess is one who is so sure of her household that she knows they will do whatever they can to make her guests comfortable.[52]

June 19, 1936, "My Day"

On Humor

[W]hen you know when to laugh and when to look upon things as too absurd to take seriously, the other person is ashamed to carry through even if he was serious about it.[53]

May 14, 1945, letter to Harry S Truman

At one point, I received a wire from Franklin: "Hope you have a good trip. What shall I do with your casket?" I puzzled over this for some time and it finally dawned on me that I had forgotten one piece of my luggage—a lunch basket! It was, of course, a typographical error, but that message remained a family joke for many years, and we told my husband he was preparing for any contingency.[54]

Circa 1949, *This I Remember*

On Individualism

Everyone must live their own life in their own way and not according to anybody else's ideas.[55]

May 15, 1933, White House press conference

It is a brave thing to do to have the courage to be an individual; it is also, perhaps a lonely thing. But it is better than not being an individual, which is to be nobody at all.[56]

Circa 1960, *You Learn by Living*

Do not ask or expect to have anyone with you on everything. Do not try for it. To reach such a state of unanimity would mean that you would risk losing your own individuality to attain it.[57]

Circa 1960, *You Learn by Living*

On Objectivity

Being objective is a matter of long training, and I am not sure that even scientists always attain it.[58]

July 26, 1944, "My Day"

On Preparedness

How hard it is for human beings to learn that the only safety there is lies in being prepared for any eventuality.[59]

December 9, 1941, "My Day"

On Propriety

No one can live according to some other person's conception of what is proper.[60]

September 4, 1943, *Cairns Post* (Cairns, Australia)

On Self-Confidence

No one can make you feel inferior without your consent.[61]

September 1940, *Reader's Digest*

First you must remember that there is a fine line between being too aggressive and being confident in your own ability.[62]

June 28, 1940, *New York Times*

To do anything constructive or creative in this world, people must have some self-confidence. Therefore people who love them must always be careful even in giving their honest criticism and opinions, not to destroy completely an individual's faith in his own judgment![63]

November 1944, *Ladies' Home Journal*

On Self-Control

Good taste may be a matter of environment but the ability to govern one's self has to be cultivated from early youth.[64]

June 1931, *Parents* magazine

Anyone who does not have enough self-control to live within the bonds of moderation is a slave in the very truest sense of the word.[65]

Circa 1946, *If You Ask Me*

On Self-Discipline

[T]he discipline one imposes on oneself is the only sure bulwark one has against fear.[66]

Circa 1960, *You Learn by Living*

Discipline of mind and body is one of the most difficult things one has to acquire, but in the long run it is a valuable ingredient of education and a tremendous bulwark in time of trouble.[67]

Circa 1960, *You Learn by Living*

Actually when you come to understand self-discipline you begin to understand the limits of freedom.[68]

Circa 1960, *You Learn by Living*

On Self-Knowledge

[P]eople seem to fear self-knowledge because they assume, and often quite wrongly, that it implies discovering only derogatory things about oneself. Actually an important part of self-knowledge is that it gives one better realization of the inner strength that can be called upon, of which one may be quite unaware.[69]

Circa 1960, *You Learn by Living*

No one, it seems to me, can really see his own life clearly any more than he can see himself, as his friends and enemies can, from all sides. It is a moral as well as a physical impossibility. The most one can achieve is to try to be as honest as possible.[70]

Circa 1961, *The Autobiography of Eleanor Roosevelt*

At times, of course, it is valuable in throwing light into dark places, but its danger is that one may easily tend to become self-absorbed in one's voyage of discovery and self-analysis.[71]

Circa 1961, *The Autobiography of Eleanor Roosevelt*

On Self-Respect

Without self-respect, few people are able to feel genuine respect for others.[72]

Circa 1960, *You Learn by Living*

On Self-Sacrifice

It is not fair to ask of others what you are not willing to do yourself.[73]

June 15, 1946, "My Day"

On Shyness

[T]he only way to get over it is to try to forget about yourself as a person and think only about what you can do to make the people around you have a better time.[74]

Circa 1946, *If You Ask Me*

On Strength

Strength that goes wrong is even more dangerous than weakness that goes wrong.[75]

April 28, 1959, "My Day"

On Trust

We can't take it for granted that we are the only trustworthy people in the world & we must believe in other people's intelligence & good intentions if we expect them to believe in us. That doesn't mean that we need to be weak either.[76]

February 28, 1943, letter to her daughter

If we hope to prosper, others prosper too, and if we hope to be trusted, we must trust others.[77]

January 5, 1946, "My Day"

On Unity/Cooperation

If unity is important for a nation, we must realize that it can not really exist unless we can bring about unity between the groups which make up that nation.[78]

January 24, 1942, "My Day"

The knowledge of how little you can do alone teaches you humility.[79]

Circa 1960, *You Learn by Living*

On Vision

For where there is no vision the people perish.[80]

Circa 1963, *Tomorrow Is Now*

On Values

Not to arrive at a clear understanding of one's own values is a tragic waste. You have missed the whole point of what life is for.[81]

Circa 1960, *You Learn by Living*

Eleanor Roosevelt, 1911. Courtesy of the Franklin D. Roosevelt Library and Museum.

13 ✻ On Emotions

Growing up during the Victorian era, Eleanor Roosevelt was trained to control her emotions. She was not allowed to cry in public and was admonished to think of the emotional needs of others before her own.[1] As a result, ER was seldom demonstrative with her affections with family or close friends.

Despite this repressive upbringing, ER showed a great capacity for love and a deep empathy for others.[2] She valued emotions as a useful tool that could be used to spur individuals to make a positive contribution to society.

✻

Perhaps it isn't such a bad thing when your emotions are stirred in the right direction, to have them become a well-spring of action.[3]

February 23, 1943, "My Day"

To live deeply requires a capacity for feeling—and that too, is something which must be developed. For the most part people's emotions, when untrained and uncontrolled are apt only to stir the surface and not to reflect themselves in thought and action.[4]

January 7, 1948, "My Day"

On Anger

It is curious how at such times one's anxiety for the nation and one's personal anxiety merge as one goes over and over all the things that have happened and may happen. For a woman, the personal side comes more strongly to the fore.[5]

Circa 1949, *This I Remember*, reflecting on Pearl Harbor Day

On Fear

A sane people, living in an atmosphere of fearlessness, does not suddenly become hysterical at the threat of invasion, even from more credible sources, let alone by the Martians from another planet, but we have allowed ourselves to be fed on propaganda which has created a fear complex.[6]

January 1939, *Virginia Quarterly Review*, reaction to hysteria in response to the *War of the Worlds* radio broadcast about a Martian invasion

Fear can take away from you all the courage to be an individual. You become a mouthpiece of ideas which you have been told you must give forth.[7]

April 1, 1950, address to the Americans for Democratic Action

Fear has always seemed to me to be the worst stumbling block which anyone has to face. It is the greatest crippler.[8]

Circa 1960, *You Learn by Living*

You gain strength, courage, and confidence by every experience in which you really stop to look fear in the face.[9]

Circa 1960, *You Learn by Living*

You must do the thing you think you cannot do.[10]

Circa 1960, *You Learn by Living*

No matter how hard hit you are, you can face what has to be faced if you have learned to master your own fears.[11]

Circa 1960, *You Learn by Living*

People who "view with alarm" never build anything.[12]

Circa 1963, *Tomorrow Is Now*

The answer to fear is not to cower and hide; it is not to surrender feebly without contest. The answer is to stand and face it boldly. Look at it, analyze it, and, in the end, act. With action, confidence grows.[13]

Circa 1963, *Tomorrow Is Now*

On Hope

Surely, in the light of history, it is more intelligent to hope rather than to fear, to try rather than not to try. For one thing we know beyond all doubt: Nothing has ever been achieved by the person who says, "It can't be done."[14]

Circa 1960, *You Learn by Living*

For men cannot live without hope. If it is not engendered by their own convictions or desires, it can easily be fired from without, and by the most meretricious and empty of promises.[15]

Circa 1961, *The Autobiography of Eleanor Roosevelt*

On Love

I solemnly answered "yes," and yet I know now that it was years before I understood what being in love or what loving really meant.[16]

Circa 1937, *This Is My Story*, reminiscence of her 1904 acceptance of FDR's marriage proposal

Love is a queer thing, it hurts but it gives one so much more in return![17]

February 4, 1934, letter to Lorena Hickok

What a nuisance hearts are & yet without them life would hardly be worthwhile.[18]

February 1, 1935, letter to Lorena Hickok

[L]ove can't be pigeon holed & perhaps we love people more for their weakness than for their best qualities.[19]

November 13, 1936, letter to Lorena Hickok

We can establish no real trust between nations until we acknowledge the power of love above all other power.[20]

Circa 1938, "This Troubled World"

It takes courage to love, but pain through love is the purifying fire which those who love generously know.[21]

April 1, 1939, "My Day"

Real loving means work, thinking of each other day in and day out, unselfishness, and effort to understand the growth of the soul and mind of the other individual, and to adjust and complement that other person day by day.[22]

October 20, 1939, "My Day"

Keeping up romance, keeping up constant interest in each other by meticulous care for the little things which were important when you were in love, this is all a part of loving.[23]

October 20, 1939, "My Day"

I don't believe distance lessens love, not if you keep feeling the people you love are always with you.[24]

May 30, 1943, letter to Joseph P. Lash

Great love, which keeps people in one's mind & heart all the time, can I think increase your understanding & devotion in spite of being apart. You suffer more because you miss people more but if it is worth loving at all it is the only real & enduring way to love.[25]

June 8, 1943, letter to Joseph P. Lash

I guess one of the sad things in life is that rarely do a man & woman fall *equally* in love with each other & even more rarely do they so live their lives that they continue to be lovers at times & still develop & enjoy constant companionship of married life.[26]

December 25, 1943, letter to Joseph P. Lash

Every woman wants to be first to someone sometime in her life & the desire is the explanation for many strange things women do, if only men understood it![27]

January 21, 1944, letter to Joseph P. Lash

It is obviously true that the first flush of being "in love" always changes into something deeper and calmer, or more superficial. I have known only a few very happy marriages. By that I do not mean just people who get along together and live contentedly through life, but people who are really excitingly happy.[28]

February 8, 1944, "My Day"

Love will have its say even under difficulties.[29]

February 29, 1944, "My Day"

Love must be given freely and not look for any return, it is only pride that makes one crave a return.[30]

Circa 1957

You like to respect and admire someone whom you love, but actually you often love even more the people who require understanding and who make mistakes and have to grow with their mistakes.[31]

March 29, 1958, "My Day"

Gratitude and love are not to be had for the asking; they are not to be bought.[32]

Circa 1961, *The Autobiography of Eleanor Roosevelt*

The basic test of friendship or love lies in the extent to which the well-being of the friend or loved one is of greater importance than one's own desires.[33]

Circa 1962, *Eleanor Roosevelt's Book of Common Sense Etiquette*

On Loneliness

[E]verything loses interest if you feel you are alone in the world and nobody cares what you do.[34]

November 22, 1943, "My Day"

[I]f I feel depressed I go to work. Work is always an antidote for depression, and loneliness is just one of the manifestations of this frame of mind.[35]

Circa 1946, *If You Ask Me*

On Pride

[T]he greatest fineness . . . is the ability to minimize your own importance even to yourself.[36]

July 28, 1936, "My Day"

On Respect

Or, instead of love, perhaps the better word would be respect. That, I think, is a noble word, an indication of a certain attitude toward one's fellow men. Used too often in a subservient sense, it is more properly a token of equality.[37]

Circa 1960, *You Learn by Living*

What we should seek, rather than gratitude or love, is the respect of the world.[38]

Circa 1961, *The Autobiography of Eleanor Roosevelt*

On Unhappiness, Sorrow, and Grief

I sometimes think that the lives of many burdens are not really to be pitied for at least they live deeply and from their sorrows spring up flowers but an empty life is really dreadful![39]

Circa 1916

Isn't it a strange world, tragedies on every side in life and death and yet so much kindness, goodness and helpfulness that one knows it must all be for some worthwhile end.[40]

Circa February 1920

It is a curious thing in human experience, but to live through a period of stress and sorrow with other human beings creates a bond which nothing seems to break. People can be happy together and look back on their contacts very pleasantly, but such contacts will not make the same kind of bond that sorrow lived together will create.[41]

Circa 1937, *This is My Story*

Even from life's sorrows some good must come.[42]

June 28, 1939, "My Day"

[Y]ou can't help [but] suffer when all the rest of the world is suffering.[43]

September 27, 1939, White House press conference

We cannot remove sorrow or disappointment from the lives of human beings, but we can give them an opportunity to free themselves from mass restrictions made by man.[44]

Circa 1940, "The Moral Basis of Democracy"

Probably the best thing that can happen to anyone at a time of personal loss is to be drawn back to work by a job that has to be done. If something must be done that requires concentration, that takes the individual out of himself, it is the best antidote for grief that I know.[45]

September 11, 1941, "My Day"

Sorrow in itself and the loss of someone whom you love is hard to bear, but when sorrow is mixed with regret and a consciousness of waste there is added a touch of bitterness which is even more difficult to carry day in and day out.[46]

Circa 1949, *This I Remember*

Unhappiness is an inward, not an outward thing.[47]

Circa 1960, *You Learn by Living*

Self-pity and withdrawal from the battle are the beginning of misery.[48]

Circa 1960, *You Learn by Living*

On Worry

It is foolish to worry, for all of us know that whatever comes we have to meet it.[49]

August 16, 1941, "My Day"

14 ❈ On Relationships

Eleanor Roosevelt treasured her relationships with family and friends. These people brought her comfort in times of trouble, trust when she needed to confide in someone, and companionship when her very public life seemed poised to overwhelm her. She believed that if the personal elements of friendship were extended to other nations, peace would ensue.

ER's sexuality has been the subject of great debate in recent years. She married FDR, and together they raised five children. Their intimate life likely changed when ER uncovered his affair with Lucy Mercer as well as when he became debilitated by polio. Some have speculated that she engaged in extramarital relationships. Friends expressed concern about her rapport with bodyguard Earl Miller, and later with Dr. David Gurewitsch.[1] She was also close to a number of women, including known lesbians Nancy Cook and Marion Dickerman. ER's letters to the reporter Lorena Hickok have been the subject of much speculation.[2] Were the two women intimate, or were their expressions of affection toward each other a holdover from an earlier time?

Letters, interviews with family and friends, and photographs hint at clandestine relationships, but there is not enough definitive evidence to support any one theory. Whether ER was monogamous or not, heterosexual, bisexual, or a lesbian, her private intimate life will likely remain private.

The Roosevelt family with children: Anna, James, Elliott, Franklin Jr., John, and Eleanor's mother-in-law, Sara, 1919. Courtesy of the Franklin D. Roosevelt Library and Museum.

On Friends and Friendship

[I]t is probably the sense of being really needed and wanted which gives us the greatest satisfaction and creates the most lasting bond.[3]

Circa 1937, *This Is My Story*

I believe that every human being needs an opportunity now and then to tell someone their passing emotions and thoughts which may have been pent up and therefore disturbing. If things have annoyed you, they fade into insignificance if you laugh about them with someone else; real sorrows even are lightened and joys are heightened in being shared.[4]

Circa 1938, *My Days*

Even in private life one of the most important things, after one's family relationship, is one's friends.[5]

August 3, 1945, "My Day"

It seems to be so easy for many people to express their enmity and so difficult to express their pleasure or friendship.[6]

August 3, 1945, "My Day"

[I]t would do us good every now and then to contemplate our friends and always to forget our enemies.[7]

August 3, 1945, "My Day"

There is no more precious experience in life than friendship. And I am not forgetting love and marriage as I write this; the lovers, or the man and wife, who are not friends are but weakly joined together. One enlarges his circle of friends through contact with many people. One who limits those contacts narrows the circle and frequently his own point of view as well.[8]

Circa 1962, *Eleanor Roosevelt's Book of Common Sense Etiquette*

Friendship with oneself is all important because without it, one cannot be friends with anyone else in the world.[9]

November 1944, *Ladies' Home Journal*

No relationship in this world ever remains warm and close unless a real effort is made on both sides to keep it so. Human relationships, like life itself, can never remain static. They grow or they diminish. But, in either case, they change. To be able to build new relations is as important as to hold the old ones, though sometimes one is obliged to sever old relationships.[10]

Circa 1960, *You Learn by Living*

[My] satisfaction is not in politics, not in the interesting things I do. It is in being with people I am fond of and feeling that in some small way I can make life happier and more interesting for them, or help them to achieve their objective. To me that is more important than anything else in my life.[11]

Circa 1960, *You Learn by Living*

[T]he most important thing in any relationship is not what you get but what you give.[12]

Circa 1937, *This Is My Story*

I know that in my own case my friends are responsible for much that I have become and without them there are many things which would have remained closed books to me.[13]

Circa 1937, *This Is My Story*

Enemies have never seemed to me very important. They can only make life disagreeable for a time, but friends can be a daily joy and an unending one.[14]

August 3, 1945, "My Day"

To have a friend who knows you by name gives you a sense that you are not alone in the world.[15]

April 23, 1962, "My Day"

Many people will walk in and out of our life, but only true friends will leave footprints in your heart.[16]

Date unknown

On Marriage

I think we must all agree that in the wife's job there are three fundamentals—being a partner, being a mother, and being a housekeeper and homemaker. Formerly, if we had been arranging the phases of the job in the order of their importance, I think we would have put being a mother first and next being a housekeeper and homemaker, and then being a partner. But today we understand that everything else depends upon the success of the wife and husband in their personal partner relationship. So from the modern point of view that comes first.[17]

Circa 1930

You may count your marriage a success as far as your husband is concerned if you feel that you are useful to him in whatever is the most engrossing interest in his life.[18]

December 1931, *Pictorial Review*

Ten Rules for Success in Marriage:

1 Have a plan, some central idea, as definite a pattern for your life as possible, and a clearly understood object for the joint project.

2 Remember that sooner or later money is apt to be a cause of friction. Keeping a budget is a practical way of eliminating the irritations and dissatisfactions that come to married people over the outlay of money.

3 Apportion your time and energy, allowing each his share of the joint home-making duties, as well as for individual responsibilities.

4 Let neither husband nor wife strive to be the dominating person in the household. A victory for either in this respect means failure of the partnership.

5 Expect to disagree. Two people may hold entirely different views on many subjects and yet respect and care for each other just the same.

6 Be honest. Each must be honest with himself and with the other, not trying to think and be things he is not.

7 Be loyal. Keep your differences to yourselves. The less said about your married troubles, except between yourselves, the better. The feeling that many young married people have, that they can complain to their parents when things do not go just right is bad for them and brings more serious trouble later on.

8 Talk things over. When hurt do not keep it to yourself, brooding over it. Meet every situation in the open. Troubles that seem momentous quickly vanish when frankly dealt with.

9 Avoid trivial criticism. Grumbling and complaints use up the vital forces of man or women.

10 Keep alive the spirit of courtship, that thoughtfulness which existed before marriage.[19]

December 1931, *Pictorial Review*

[N]o two people really know each other until they have been married for some time.[20]

December 1937, *Good Housekeeping*

The happiness of husband and wife is often wrecked by too little dependence on each other, for to be happy two people must need each other in everything they do.[21]

December 1937, *Good Housekeeping*

I think we ought to impress on both our girls and boys that successful marriage requires just as much work, just as much intelligence and just as much unselfish devotion, as they give to any position they undertake to fill on a paid basis.[22]

March 29, 1941, "My Day"

I have known only a few very happy marriages. By that I do not mean just people who get along together and live contentedly through life, but people who really are excitingly happy. These people have somehow preserved the ability to rejuvenate their love so that neither the man nor the woman need wander off to find the romance they long for somewhere else.[23]

February 8, 1944, "My Day"

All human beings have failings, all human beings have needs and temptations and stresses. Men and women who live together through long years get to know one another's failings; but they also come to know what is worthy of respect and admiration in those they live with and in themselves.[24]

Circa 1949, *This I Remember*

I imagine that the really great number of men & women who are faithful to each other not only in deed but in thought are so more often because of the lack of opportunity for romance elsewhere than because they've learned the secret of "the one & only great love."[25]

December 25, 1943, letter to Joseph P. Lash

I think people are happier in marriage when neither one is the boss, but when both of them are willing to give as well as take.[26]

Circa 1946, *If You Ask Me*

That he shall be honest, not only in material things, but in intellectual things; that he shall be capable of real love; and that he shall find the world an increasingly interesting place in which to live every day of his life.[27]

Circa 1946, *If You Ask Me,* on qualities of a good husband

A marriage without love is intolerable, and a home without love is a poor place for a child to grow up. Every child needs a home and security, but it is impossible to have any security or any real home when love does not exist between father and mother.[28]

Circa 1946, *If You Ask Me*

[H]appy marriages develop when the man shows his desire to the woman and she responds fully and happily.[29]

Circa 1949

Remember dear, marriages are two-way streets and when they are happy *both* must be willing to adjust. Both *must* love.[30]

Circa fall 1951, advice to David Gurewitsch

I am sure that the number of unhappy marriages and divorces would decrease sharply if only the so common program of falling in love first and then learning to know each other were reversed.[31]

Circa 1962, *Eleanor Roosevelt's Book of Common Sense Etiquette*

On Divorce

Today many seem to think that marriage is like a position in employment, which one can leave when everything does not go well. We should think of it as a permanent, lifetime job.[32]

December 1931, *Pictorial Review*

[B]etter that a home should be broken than that the children should live where their father and mother are continually pulling against each other.[33]

December 1931, *Pictorial Review*

[C]ertainly, if two people no longer love each other that is sufficient cause for divorce.[34]

Circa 1946, *If You Ask Me*

On Polygamy

[T]hough Moslem law permits a man to have four wives, it stipulates that he may not favor one at the expense of the others. (I gather for the Moslem ladies to whom I talked that a trend toward monogamy was definitely indicated, since, under present conditions it was going to be increasingly difficult to persuade four women that they were all being treated equally well.)[35]

Circa 1953, *India and the Awakening East*

On Parenting

As parents, we must realize that modern life tends to make us soft, and we must let our children meet their own difficulties, find their own solutions to knotty problems and gain experience in themselves.[36]

June 1931, *Parent's Magazine*

Nothing is more pathetic than a bored child; and one becomes bored when there is nothing new that is of interest. So open up all the avenues of rich experience to your children and encourage them to follow them for themselves.[37]

June 1931, *Parent's Magazine*

It is better to allow too much freedom than too little. . . . It is better for them to get their feet wet than to be told at the age of fifteen to put on their rubbers.[38]

Circa 1933, *It's Up to the Women*

I learned early that children leave home and lead lives of their own and that it is well not to cling to them too much, for that is sometimes the surest way of losing them altogether.[39]

Circa 1937, *This Is My Story*

[H]aving children is, perhaps, the beginning of an education for them, but it is certainly the beginning of an education for the parents.[40]

November 11, 1938, "My Day"

Our great trouble is that we tend to bring up our children for the world in which we ourselves have lived. We rarely take into consideration the changes which have come about in our own lifetime and which are likely to come about before our children are fully grown. Perhaps we handicap them unnecessarily by too much anchoring to the old and too little preparation for the new.[41]

July 7, 1942, "My Day"

I should like to have mothers everywhere recognize that their responsibility to their children, which they so often think is limited to physical and moral care, is really never fully carried out unless they fulfill their responsibility as citizens.[42]

May 15, 1945, "My Day"

I do not think that any girl who does not wish to have children should expect to marry. . . . If a girl is strong and well, the bearing of children is a privilege and the natural expression of the love of two people for each other.[43]

Circa 1946, *If You Ask Me*

One of the problems all parents face is that of bringing up their children to be as free of fear as possible. Certainly you can't accomplish this unless you have developed a philosophy for yourself that is freed of fear. If you can give them a trust in God, they will have one sure way of meeting all the uncertainties of existence.[44]

Circa 1960, *You Learn by Living*

The children will accept the standards their parents have set as examples. But, if it is all talk, if the parents say one thing and do another, the children will be antagonistic and will care nothing about what their parents want them to do.[45]

Circa 1960, *You Learn by Living*

The child who is aware that his parents do not tell him the truth will assume that the practical method is to lie. The child who sees his parents sacrifice everything for material possessions will not believe that spiritual values are important.[46]

Circa 1960, *You Learn by Living*

I was so concerned with bringing up my children properly that I was not wise enough to love them. Now, looking back, I think I would rather spoil a child a little and have more fun out of it.[47]

Circa 1961, *The Autobiography of Eleanor Roosevelt*

Daughters will be grateful and remember all their lives the things which their father introduced them to: gentleness and thoughtfulness and appreciation of themselves as women. These are qualities which, someday, they will look for in their maturity.[48]

Circa 1960, *You Learn by Living*

If you live what you believe, your children will believe it too.[49]

Circa 1960, *You Learn by Living*

Eleanor Roosevelt firing a hand gun at Chazy Lake, New York, 1934. Courtesy of the Franklin D. Roosevelt Library and Museum.

15 ✳ Miscellaneous

On Admiration

You always admire what you really don't understand.[1]
September 16, 1956, *Meet the Press*, NBC Television

On Airplanes and Air Travel

As I have never been aloft, I would like to take a flight in it. In fact, . . . no flight, no christening.[2]
June 10, 1929, *Time*, tongue-in-cheek request to fly in a new test plane

It was like being on top of the world![3]
April 21, 1933, *New York Times*, on her ride with Amelia Earhart

[A]fter the war we will have planes as manageable as any car, and which can land in a field by your cottage in the country or on the roof of your city apartment.[4]
July 17, 1944, "My Day"

On Billboards

They really spoil the landscape and somehow it seems our ingenuity should find a way to attract our attention to our wares without this particular type of advertising.[5]
March 2, 1936, "My Day"

On Birth Control

The Creator gave the power to human beings to continue their species on this earth, but he also gave them minds for use.[6]

Circa 1946, *If You Ask Me*

On Change

I think I'm pretty much a fatalist. You have to accept whatever comes and the only important thing is that you meet it with courage and with the best that you have to give.[7]

Circa 1950

You can't move so fast that you try to change the mores faster than people can accept it. That doesn't mean you do nothing, but it means that you do the things that need to be done according to priority.[8]

Circa 1956

But to force anything upon an individual is rarely successful in helping him to develop his own individuality.[9]

Circa 1960, *You Learn by Living*

In a sense nearly all great civilizations that perished did so because they had crystallized, because they were incapable of adapting themselves to new conditions, new methods, new points of view. It is as though people would literally rather die than change.[10]

Circa 1963, *Tomorrow Is Now*

On Charity

It is nice to hand out milk and bread. It gives you a comfortable feeling inside. But fundamentally you are not relieving the whole problem of the reasons why we have to have this charity.[11]

January 13, 1932, *New York Times*

Nothing should be done to make children feel themselves objects of charity.[12]

December 20, 1938, *New York Times*

Down deep in all of us, there is a desire to give as well as to receive.[13]

July 23, 1941, "My Day"

I would rather give money, on the chance of sometimes giving unwisely, than to withhold it from some one person who might need a helping hand and deserves it.[14]

Circa 1946, *If You Ask Me*

I do not question that I often gave to people who were not worthy; but in those years it seemed better to take that risk than to fail those who were worthy.[15]

Circa 1949, *This I Remember*, on her giving during the Depression

On Choices

In our country we must trust the people to hear and see both the good and the bad and choose the good.[16]

October 29, 1947, "My Day"

One's philosophy is not best expressed in words; it is expressed in the choices one makes.[17]

Circa 1960, *You Learn by Living*

In the long run, we shape our lives, and we shape ourselves. The process never ends until we die. And the choices we make are ultimately our own responsibility.[18]

Circa 1960, *You Learn by Living*

We all create the person we become by our choices as we go through life. In a very real sense, by the time we are adults, we are the sum total of the choices we have made.[19]

Circa 1960, *You Learn by Living*

On Community

[U]nless one becomes some part of community life, there comes a day when life ceases to have much interest. There are many times when thinking only of one's own affairs is so very dull.[20]

March 5, 1942, "My Day"

On Compromise

Compromises are never satisfactory. They are always the half-way measures which really please no one.[21]

May 8, 1945, "My Day"

On Convictions

It is always disagreeable to take stands. It is always easier to compromise, always easier to let things go. To many women, and I am one of them, it is extraordinarily difficult to care about anything enough to cause disagreement or unpleasant feelings, but I have come to the conclusion that this must be done for a time until we can prove our strength and demand respect for our wishes.[22]

April 1924, speech given to the women's dinner at the New York Democratic Convention

Young or old, in order to be useful we must stand for the things we feel are right, and we must work for those things wherever we find ourselves. It does very little good to believe something unless you tell your friends and associates of your beliefs.[23]

May 7, 1945, "My Day"

In the long run there is no more liberating, no more exhilarating experience than to determine one's position, state it bravely, and then *act boldly*.[24]

Circa 1963, *Tomorrow Is Now*

On Crime

I have always had a feeling that society ought to look with more disfavor on the man who profits from other people's crimes than on the criminals themselves.[25]

August 26, 1942, "My Day"

On Criticism

It's well to be critical of ourselves, or the things we do, but always to be critical with the object of finding something better—not just to tear down but to suggest and to experiment with doing something better.[26]

March 1941, *Common Sense*

Destructive criticism is always valueless and anyone with common sense soon becomes completely indifferent to it.[27]

November 1944, *Ladies' Home Journal*

My dear boy I only say these things for your own good[.] I have found in [a] lifetime of adversity that when blows are rained on one, it is advisable to turn the other profile.[28]

January 29, 1959, telegram to John F. Kennedy

Curiously enough, it is often the people who refuse to assume any responsibility who are apt to be the sharpest critics of those who do.[29]

Circa 1960, *You Learn by Living*

On Danger

In my own case, at least, it was not a sign of courage that I went ahead and did certain things which might have had some slight danger attached to them. It was simply that, like most human beings, I am not given to seeing myself disappear off the face of the earth.[30]

Circa 1949, *This I Remember*

One can fight danger only when one is armed with solid facts and spurred on by an unwavering faith and determination.[31]

Circa 1961, *The Autobiography of Eleanor Roosevelt*

On the Daughters of the American Revolution

One might hope that an organization such as the Daughters of the American Revolution would have the courage to stand alone. . . . [T]hey must be conscious of their Revolutionary ancestry, who came as immigrants to this country to escape discrimination in other lands.[32]

October 15, 1945, "My Day." ER hoped in vain that the D.A.R. would reconsider its 1939 refusal to allow African American contralto Marian Anderson to perform at their hall.

When I was in Washington they were an extremely narrow and conservative group of people, with a great fear of anything new. They still, I fear, have these same characteristics, but that doesn't prevent them from doing excellent patriotic service in the preservation of historical landmarks throughout the country.[33]

September 1953, *McCall's Magazine*

On Duty

One can be personally indifferent & yet do one's duty. As a matter of fact it is only when one is oneself very unhappy that one ever thinks about the individual right to the pursuit of happiness. When you reach my age, it comes less & less often.[34]

August 3, 1936, letter to Lorena Hickok

On Ethics

If a thing is right and you work at it, you will ultimately be helped by something stronger than yourself.[35]

October 10, 1954, *New York Times*

On Example

Example is the best lesson there is.[36]

Circa 1963, *Tomorrow Is Now*

On Failure

After all, there's no real reason why you should fail. Just stop thinking about yourself.[37]

Circa 1960, *You Learn by Living*

Life teaches you that you cannot attain real maturity until you are ready to accept this harsh knowledge [of your] limitation in yourself, and make the difficult adjustment.[38]

Circa 1960, *You Learn by Living*

No man is defeated without until he has first been defeated within.[39]

Circa 1960, *You Learn by Living*

On Fashion

Was I? I didn't know it.[40]

On hearing she was the best-dressed American woman for 1934

Buy because the thing suits you and your own taste, not simply because it is in style.[41]

April 5, 1945, *New York Times*

Slacks are nice for lounging at home, they are good for certain kinds of outdoor activities, but I think they should not be worn universally.[42]

Circa 1946, *If You Ask Me*

The woman who dresses to suit her particular type, with only a moderate bowing acquaintance with fashion, comes out better than the woman who is a slave to the designer of the moment.[43]

December 3, 1954, "My Day"

On the Future

The future belongs to those who believe in the beauty of their dreams.[44]

Circa 1954

I can think of a thousand things in the past for which I am deeply thankful, but it is for the future really that I am most grateful—for the chance to try again to build a decent world; for the young people who are so much better educated in world affairs than we were twenty-odd years ago, and who have high hopes and visions, but who stand foursquare and face the realities of life.[45]

November 26, 1942, "My Day"

Perhaps the new frontier today is something more than the revolution in textiles and methods and speed and goods. It is the frontier of men's minds. But we cannot cast an enduring light on other men's minds unless the light in our own minds burns with a hard, unquenchable flame.[46]

Circa 1961, *The Autobiography of Eleanor Roosevelt*

It is a new industrial revolution that we are pioneering. The eyes of the world are on us. If we do it badly we will be criticized and our way of life downgraded. If we do it well we can become a beacon light for the future of the world.[47]

Circa 1961, *The Autobiography of Eleanor Roosevelt*

What we must learn to do is to create unbreakable bonds between the sciences and the humanities. We cannot procrastinate. The world of the future is in our making.[48]

Circa 1963, *Tomorrow Is Now*

The future is literally in our hands to mold as we like. But we cannot wait until tomorrow. Tomorrow is now.[49]

Circa 1963, *Tomorrow Is Now*

On the Handicapped

The crippled child needs even more than the normal child. They need the ability to rely on themselves.[50]

October 5, 1933, White House press conference

We must give them the feeling that we are still dependent upon them, for if we do not do this we will kill the thing in them that makes life worth while.[51]

September 22, 1943, *New York Times*, call to support injured war veterans

On Health

If a whole community does not live under sanitary conditions, no one in the community is entirely safe.[52]

December 4, 1944, "My Day," justification for public health initiatives

Without health no nation can successfully defend itself against the aggression of other nations, either in the military or the economic field.[53]

September 1945

Our doctors had better start finding out why men wear out faster than women and they had better keep them alive for the happiness and contentment of all.[54]

May 13, 1955, "My Day"

On the Home and Homemaking

To make a house a home is still the greatest gift a woman has to give. To make a home under any and all conditions, with whatever is at hand, is genius.[55]

May 14, 1933, *New York Times*

Few seem capable of realizing that the real reason that home is important is that it is so closely tied, by a million strings, to the rest of the world.[56]

August 24, 1935, *Saturday Evening Post*

There are moments when I wish we had always lived like birds, made our own nests and needed no furnishings![57]

February 17, 1942, "My Day," her reaction to moving after the death of FDR

I think houses like to be lived in. Something happens to them when they are left empty too long. An old house will have a very distinct atmosphere, and houses which are loved and lived in by people who express themselves in their surroundings, grow to have a real personality.[58]

February 29, 1944, "My Day"

One thing is certain: in this modern world of ours we cannot afford to forget that what we do at home is important in relation to the rest of the world.[59]

Circa 1963, *Tomorrow Is Now*

On Judging People

We have long held in this country that ability should be the criterion on which all people are judged. It seems to me that we must come to recognize that this criterion in dealing with all human beings, and not place any limitations upon their achievements except such as may be imposed by their own character and intelligence.[60]

January 1936, *Opportunity*

I have gradually come to believe that human beings who try to judge other human beings are undertaking a somewhat difficult job. When your duty does not thrust ultimate judgments upon you, perhaps it is well to keep an open and charitable mind, and to try to understand why people do things instead of condemning the acts themselves.[61]

Circa 1937, *This Is My Story*

On Justice

Justice cannot be for one side alone, but must be for both.[62]

October 14, 1947, "My Day"

On Language

The fact that the Russians can show such unity and strength, and still speak 100 different languages, has shaken my faith a little in the efficacy of teaching all the peoples of the world one language in the interests of peace.[63]

December 4, 1943, "My Day"

Language is so important. It's built on the customs and beliefs of people. It's a reflection of a society; even humor is different from nation to nation.[64]

Circa 1945

On Leadership

Leaders must have faith in themselves, but their real strength comes when they trust to the guidance of a higher power than their own.[65]

September 8, 1944, "My Day"

[T]he Almighty is trying to show us that a leader may chart the way, may point out the road to lasting peace, but that many leaders and many peoples must do the building. It cannot be the work of one man, nor can the responsibility be laid upon his shoulders, and so, when the time comes for peoples to assume the burden more fully, he is given rest.[66]

April 17, 1945, "My Day," following the death of FDR

Great leaders we have had, but we could not have had great leaders unless they had a great people to follow.[67]

August 13, 1956, address to the Democratic National Convention

I have complete faith in the American people's ability if they know and if they have leadership. No one can move without some leadership.[68]

November 23, 1957, interview by Mike Wallace

A leader must not get too far ahead or he will outdistance his followers; but he must move at least a step ahead.[69]

Circa 1960, *You Learn by Living*

On Leisure

[For] if man is to be liberated to enjoy more leisure, he must also be prepared to enjoy this leisure fully and creatively. For people to have more time to read, to take part in their civic obligations, to know more about how their government functions and who their officials are might mean in a democracy a great improvement in the democratic process.[70]

November 5, 1958, "My Day"

If the use of leisure time is confined to looking at TV for a few extra hours a day, we will deteriorate as a people.[71]

November 5, 1958, "My Day"

The President has warned that we are becoming a nation of spectators rather than partakers. If our added leisure means watching baseball and football on television, with no real occupation in which we put our own brains and energies to work, then I must join the President in his exhortation to begin to do things, not just watch things being done.[72]

December 13, 1961, "My Day"

On Librarians

[I] could not help but wish that more people could realize the unselfish services that the librarians, throughout the country, have performed during the past few years. In the face of salary cuts and decreased appropriations for books, they have carried on and made their libraries a refuge and center for many people who sorely needed friendly contacts. I am more and more impressed as I grow older by the unsung heroes of the world, and wish that some one would write an epic about those who carry the brunt of the world's work on their shoulders, receiving little attention in return.[73]

April 3, 1936, "My Day"

On Life

The life you live is your own.[74]

Circa 1919

Life is meant to be lived.[75]

Circa 1919

Life has gradually taught me to be adaptable, never to make an issue of little things, to remember that the objective is important but not to force everybody else into your own pattern.[76]

February 4, 1936, "My Day"

Life seems full of the unexpected. Just as you think everything is serene around you it seems to be necessary to remind you that everything is uncertain and that life should always be lived with the feeling that this may be one's last day on earth![77]

July 28, 1936, "My Day," on the death of a secret service agent assigned to her family

The things that happen in life are not so important as what they do to people, and that is what makes them of such extraordinary interest. I don't think most people leave happy lives.[78]

February 25, 1937, *New York Times*

It's a great life if you never get tired![79]

January 25, 1936, "My Day"

When life is too easy for us, we must beware or we may not be ready to meet the blows which sooner or later come to everyone, rich or poor.[80]

February 23, 1940, "My Day"

It is only the knowledge that you are fighting for a better future which makes life worth living.[81]

March 1941, *Common Sense*

You can never really live anyone else's life, not even your child's. The influence you exert is through your own life, and what you've become yourself.[82]

Circa 1941

I say to the young, "Do not stop thinking of life as an adventure. You have no security unless you can live bravely, excitingly, imaginatively."[83]

Circa 1961, *The Autobiography of Eleanor Roosevelt*

It's your life—but only if you make it so. The standards by which you live must be your own standards, your own values, your own conviction in regard to what is right and wrong, what is true and false, what is important and what is trivial. When you adopt the standards and values of someone else or a community or a pressure group, you surrender your own integrity. You become, to the extent of your surrender, less of a human being.[84]

Circa 1960, *You Learn by Living*

Your life is your own. You mold it. You make it.[85]

Circa 1960, *You Learn by Living*

Life was meant to be lived, and curiosity must be kept alive. One must never, for whatever reason, turn his back on life.[86]

Circa 1961, *The Autobiography of Eleanor Roosevelt*

No man has ever known what he would meet around the next corner; if life were predictable it would cease to be life, and be without flavor.[88]

Circa 1963, *Tomorrow Is Now*

On Manners

I think, perhaps, good manners, which really mean true kindness of heart, would help a great deal in living in a democratic way.[89]

April 12, 1943, "My Day"

Too many people have forgotten good manners and their importance in soothing and making gracious and pleasant our dealings with our fellows. I am not referring now to rigid rules of etiquette but to the simple human kindness that is the foundation of all formal politeness.[90]

Circa 1960, *You Learn by Living*

On Mistakes

When we make mistakes ourselves we hate to have other people notice them, but when the boot is on the other foot, we leave nothing unnoticed.[91]

March 4, 1936, "My Day"

We will make mistakes. But if we take them and are willing to acknowledge them and to change, that will mean that we will, in the end, succeed.[92]

Circa 1959

[P]erhaps one can learn only by one's own mistakes. The essential thing is to learn.[93]

Circa 1960, *You Learn by Living*

It is the better part of wisdom to regard the mistake as experience which will help guide you in the future, a part though a painful part, of your education. For all of us, no matter how good our training, will make bad choices. We will, through increased experience, make better choices as life goes on.[94]

Circa 1960, *You Learn by Living*

On Nature

One of the blessings of life in the rural areas is the fact that any child or adult can escape and be alone with nature at a moment's notice.[95]

June 28, 1944, "My Day"

Many years ago I learned that nature had more to give, from the healing point of view, than any human being.[96]

April 26, 1945, "My Day"

Yes, the world does live again. Perhaps nature is our best assurance of immortality.[97]

April 26, 1945, "My Day"

On Opinions

Whether you agree with everything that is said is immaterial. The point is that it is good for people to state openly what they have on their minds and in their hearts.[98]

February 26, 1940, *Life*

Only stupid people remain rigid and inflexible in their opinions and ideas.[99]

October 25, 1945, "My Day"

On Opponents

I sometimes wonder whether the writers and speakers who try to befuddle other people are really befuddled themselves![100]

November 14, 1944, "My Day," response to opponents of her husband's wartime leadership

We must be able to disagree with people, and to consider new ideas and not be afraid.[101]

Circa 1951

To refuse to know or understand the opposition seems to me madness.[102]

Circa 1961, *The Autobiography of Eleanor Roosevelt*

On Pets

[F]or there are few human bonds which mean more than the bond between a dog and his master or mistress.[103]

February 20, 1936, "My Day"

I have always felt that anyone who was really liked my dogs could be counted on to have certain decent qualities in human relationships.[104]

January 11, 1941, "My Day"

On Power

Complete power over others is not good for any of us, but with the right to use a whip it is almost sure to degrade.[105]

March 24, 1941, "My Day"

On the Press

Newspaper correspondents are no different from other human beings—they are good and bad.[106]

January 1940, *Good Housekeeping*

If you deal with the press you are apt to become slightly suspicious. Remember, it's their job to get a good story, and it's our job not to get caught.[107]

February 27, 1942, *New York Times*

From my point of view it is a satisfactory profession, if not a glamorous one.[108]

March 4, 1944, "My Day," on journalism as a career

I wonder if it isn't being a crusader to learn to give facts and to try to get the truth before the readers of a paper.[109]

March 4, 1944, "My Day"

Photographers are not accustomed to being their own victims, and I think it is probably very good for them.[110]

November 29, 1944, "My Day"

It is very difficult to have a free, fair, and honest press anywhere in the world. In the first place, as a rule, papers are largely supported by advertising, and that immediately gives the advertisers a certain hold over the medium which they use.[111]

Circa 1946, *If You Ask Me*

On Progress

[I]t is our freedom to progress that makes us all want to live and to go on.[112]

May 29, 1941, "My Day"

It is horrible that it takes a war to make us progress, nevertheless it is true that we have progressed by leaps and bounds among many lines.[113]

October 30, 1943, "My Day"

When we become satisfied, progress stops.[114]

March 16, 1947, *New York Times*

On Psychology

Psychology may be a science, but a knowledge of human nature is its basis.[115]

July 17, 1943, "My Day"

On Public Opinion

And yet the most powerful weapon that we have at our command today is public opinion. Statesmen quail before it, and it could move mountains.[116]

Circa 1938, *My Days*

On Quotations

It has always seemed to me very unwise to quote people after they are dead. . . . They can no longer speak for themselves. They can neither explain why they did or said certain things, nor give the reasons which influenced them at the time. Therefore it seems to me that using past utterances to influence new decisions is not only unfair but very unwise.[117]

October 25, 1945, "My Day"

On Secrets

Hidden things are bad and cause us a great deal more trouble than the things that are out and stated and which we know we should go to work on.[118]

February 12, 1940, White House press conference

On Simplicity

A little simplification would be the first step toward rational living, I think.[119]

February 20, 1936, "My Day"

I do not know that Gandhi's plans for living could be applied to modern life, but there is no doubt in my mind that the more we simplify our material needs the more we are free to think of other things.[120]

January 27, 1953, "My Day"

On Sins

I have often thought that so much attention is paid to the aggressive sins, such as violence and cruelty and greed with all their tragic effects, that too little attention is paid to the passive sins, such as apathy and laziness, which in the long run can have a more devastating and destructive effect upon society than the others.[121]

Circa 1960, *You Learn by Living*

On Success

Everything depends upon whether we use our privileges rightly.[122]

October 8, 1944, *New York Times*

A successful life for a man or a woman seems to me to live in the knowledge that one has developed to the limit [of] the capacities with which one was endowed; that one has contributed something constructive to family and friends and to a home community; that one has brought happiness wherever it was possible; that one has earned one's way in the world, has kept some friends, and need not be ashamed to face oneself honestly.[123]

Circa 1946, *If You Ask Me*

Your ambition should be to get as much life out of living as you possibly can, as much enjoyment, as much interest, as much experience, as much understanding. Not simply to be what is generally called a "success."[124]

Circa 1960, *You Learn by Living*

Being a success is tied up very closely with being one's own kind of individual.[125]

Circa 1960, *You Learn by Living*

Success must include two things: the development of an individual to his utmost potentiality and a contribution of some kind to one's world.[126]

Circa 1960, *You Learn by Living*

On Time

[T]he present is the only thing we really possess.[127]

September 22, 1941, "My Day"

Time is never long enough for happiness anyway.[128]

February 5, 1943, "My Day"

[U]nless time is good for something it is good for nothing.[129]

Circa 1960, *You Learn by Living*

The most unhappy people in the world are those who face the days without knowing what to do with their time.[130]

Circa 1960, *You Learn by Living*

Each of us has . . . all the time there is. Those years, weeks, hours are sands in the glass running swiftly away. To let them drift through our fingers is a tragic waste. To use them to the hilt, making them count for something, is the beginning of wisdom.[131]

Circa 1960, *You Learn by Living*

Every age is an unknown country.[132]

Circa 1963, *Tomorrow Is Now*

On Travel

Traveling is always an opportunity for me, not only to read, which is a refreshing stimulant, but also to look at the vastness of our nation and reflect upon our tremendous opportunities, which we are not yet using to full advantage.[133]

March 2, 1942, "My Day"

Perhaps, someday, travel will be so quick and easy that every country will represent people to us, people whom we know and understand.[134]

May 28, 1943, "My Day"

Actually, though, I would say that the greatest thing I have learned is how good it is to come home again.[135]

October 8, 1944, New York Times

An American traveling abroad is an ambassador not only of the United States, but also for the concept of democracy and, if he is a white American, for the entire white race. Wherever he goes, America and democracy will be thought of with a little more or a little less respect after he has departed.[136]

Circa 1962, Eleanor Roosevelt's Book of Common Sense Etiquette

On Violence

There is no doubt that we still live in a world where to a good many people force is the only voice which carries any weight.[137]

February 14, 1938, White House press conference

People must learn that force is a very destructive method of control. That reason and cooperation are the only methods by which we can build a world constructively.[138]

June 9, 1943, "My Day"

I was sick at heart when I came here, over race riots which put us on a par with Nazism which we fight, and make one tremble for what human beings may do when they no longer think but let themselves be dominated by their worst emotions.[139]

July 14, 1943, "My Day," on the Detroit race riots that left thirty-four dead and hundreds wounded

16 ☀ On Herself

Eleanor Roosevelt often fixated on her mistakes and personal shortcomings. She criticized her appearance, her choices, and what she considered was her own ignorance. This self-deprecating language may have been a preemptive strike, an attempt to take the sting out of the criticisms of others by first making them herself.

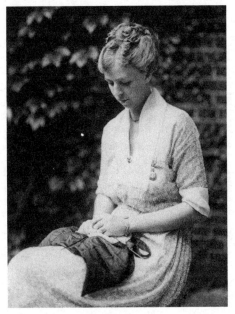

Eleanor Roosevelt, Washington, D.C., circa 1914. Courtesy of the Franklin D. Roosevelt Library and Museum.

On Her Childhood

I was a solemn child without beauty and painfully shy and I seemed like a little old woman entirely lacking in the spontaneous joy and mirth of youth.[1]

November 20, 1933, *Time*

Looking back I see that I was always afraid of something: of the dark, of displeasing people, of failure. Anything that I accomplished had to be done across a barrier of fear.[2]

Circa 1937, *This Is My Story*

As I look back, I think probably the factor which influenced me most in my early years was an avid desire, even before I was aware what I was doing, to experience all I could as deeply as I could.[3]

Circa 1960, *You Learn by Living*

On Herself

Why me? I am plain, I have little to bring you.[4]

Circa November 1903, response to FDR's proposal of marriage

I hardly think the word "passionate" applies to me.[5]

April 5, 1930, *New Yorker*, response to a reporter who referred to her "passionate interest" in welfare legislation

I don't think I'm very bright but I've been exposed to so many bright people I can pick their brains.[6]

Circa 1933

If I really had to go out and earn my own living, entirely on my own, I'd have to do it as a scrubwoman. And I'd probably not be very good at that. I have no profession—no training for anything.[7]

Circa early 1933

I'm an idiotic puritan & I wish I had the right kind of sense of humor & could enjoy certain things.[8]

November 19, 1934. As the daughter of an alcoholic, ER was uncomfortable with her family's social drinking.

Darling, don't let anyone hold memorial meetings for me after I leave you. . . . I'd like to be remembered happily if that is possible, if that can't be then I'd rather be forgotten.[9]

December 19, 1935, letter to Lorena Hickok regarding her death

I can't tell you how happy this makes me, to receive all this attention for something I have done myself and not because of Franklin.[10]

Circa 1936, on the forthcoming release of *This Is My Story*

I want everything around me in its place. Dirt or disorder makes me positively uncomfortable.[11]

Circa 1937, *This Is My Story*

I have a deep discouragement about the world these days & would like to run away from having to face it. If I feel that way what must other less secure people feel?[12]

August 11, 1940, letter to Lorena Hickok

I began to feel I was being introduced to someone I really did not know.[13]

October 23, 1940, "My Day," response to Ruby Black's book, *Eleanor Roosevelt, a Biography*

I think I approached my own motherhood with a keen sense of responsibility but very little sense of the joy which should come with having babies. It was a long time before I gained enough confidence in my own judgment really to enjoy a child. I do not know that even today I have it.[14]

June 15, 1940, *Collier's*

There is no accomplishment of mine that I think could possibly be important enough to be recorded, and I have no desire to be remembered except by the few people whom I love.[15]

Circa 1946, *If You Ask Me*

I guess I'd list myself as a housewife—with some experience in writing a column and in speaking—and that's all.[16]

March 17, 1942, *Washington Times-Herald*

Most of my life has been spent getting accustomed to doing one thing, and then finding I have to do something entirely different.[17]

July 8, 1942, "My Day"

I can forgive, but I can't forget.[18]

Circa 1945, on her daughter's role in reconnecting FDR with his mistress, Lucy Mercer Rutherfurd

Why, I don't know that I can claim any real achievements.[19]

October 8, 1944, *New York Times*

Because I was the wife of the President, certain restrictions were imposed upon me. Now I am on my own, and I hope to write as a newspaper woman.[20]

April 19, 1945, "My Day." A week after FDR's death, ER was making plans to support herself.

Long ago, as an individual, I found it was better to be fooled occasionally than always to be suspicious of other people's motives.[21]

September 28, 1945, "My Day"

For the first time in my life I can say just what I want. For your information it is wonderful to feel free.[22]

January 4, 1946, off-the-record comment made during a press conference regarding her future plans following FDR's death

I'm so glad I never feel important, it does complicate life![23]

February 2, 1946, letter to her daughter

I manage to do a lot because I am interested in my work. And besides that, it's hard to keep Roosevelts down.[24]

December 15, 1946, *New York Times Magazine*

No, I have never wanted to be a man. I have often wanted to be more effective as a woman, but I have never felt that trousers would do the trick![25]

Circa 1946, *If You Ask Me*

I can be calm and quiet, but it takes all the discipline I have acquired in life to keep on talking and smiling and to concentrate on the conversation addressed to me. I want to be left alone while I store up fortitude for what I fear may be a blow of fate. However, I have learned to feel one way inside at such times and outwardly to go on like an automation.[26]

Circa 1949, *This I Remember*

I have never known what it was to be bored or to have time hang heavily on my hands. It has always been difficult to find time to do the things I want to do.[27]

Circa 1949, *This I Remember*

I was slightly indignant, because I was unable to see how in a few weeks my blood could have changed; I realized, however that there had to be some definite limit set, and so I felt I really entered old age on October 11, 1944.[28]

Circa 1949, *This I Remember,* on being rejected as a blood donor because of being age sixty

I think I should die if I had to live in Soviet Russia.[29]

October 4, 1959, *New York Times*

About the only value the story of my life may have is to show that one can, even without any particular gifts, overcome obstacles that seem insurmountable if one is willing to face the fact that they must be overcome; in spite of timidity and fear, in spite of a lack of talents, one can find a way to live widely and fully.[30]

Circa 1961, *The Autobiography of Eleanor Roosevelt*

I had really only three assets: I was keenly interested, I accepted every challenge and every opportunity to learn more, and I had great energy and self-discipline.[31]

Circa 1961, *The Autobiography of Eleanor Roosevelt*

[H]aving learned to stare down fear, I long ago reached the point where there is no living person whom I fear, and few challenges that I am not willing to face.[32]

Circa 1961, *The Autobiography of Eleanor Roosevelt*

It is startling to realize that one is so deeply, fanatically disliked by a number of people.[33]

Circa 1961, *The Autobiography of Eleanor Roosevelt*

I think I must have a good deal of my uncle Theodore Roosevelt in me because I enjoy a good fight.[34]

Circa 1961, *The Autobiography of Eleanor Roosevelt*

I could not, at any age, be content to take my place in a corner by the fireside and simply look on.[35]

Circa 1960–61

Like the elephant's child in Kipling's story, I have an insatiable curiosity about people in general.[36]

Unknown date

Her Advice to Others

Have convictions. Be friendly. Stick to your beliefs as they stick to theirs. Work as hard as they do.[37]

Circa 1946, on how to deal with the Russians

Do the things that interest you and do them with all your heart. Don't be concerned about whether people are watching you or criticizing you. The chances are that they aren't even paying any attention to you. It's your attention to yourself that is so stultifying.[38]

Circa 1960, *You Learn by Living*

On Her Role, Influence, and Experiences as First Lady

I'm afraid that you won't have much to write about. I'll not be doing anything very interesting.[39]

Circa October 1932, remark to reporters after FDR's election

I never wanted it even though some people have said that my ambition for myself drove him on. They've even said that I had some such idea in the back of my mind when I married him. I never wanted to be a President's wife, and I don't want it now.[40]

Circa October 1932

But, there isn't going to be any First Lady of the Land. There is going to be plain, ordinary Mrs. Roosevelt. I shall very likely be criticized, but I can't help it.[41]

November 9, 1932, to the reporter Lorena Hickok

I don't suppose anybody will ever call me Eleanor anymore.[42]

Circa late 1932, after FDR was elected president

My feeling about the White House is that it belongs to the people. Their taxes support it. It is really theirs. And as far as possible, they should be made to feel welcome here. They shouldn't have the feeling that they are shut out.[43]

March 5, 1933, *New York Times*. ER was criticized for opening the White House for tours to the general public.

There is, however, one consolation to any one who lives in the public eye, namely, that while it may be most difficult to keep the world from knowing where you dine and what you eat and what you wear, so much interest is focused on these somewhat unimportant things, that you are really left completely free to live your own inner life as you wish.[44]

January 7, 1936, "My Day"

[T]he more you live in a "gold-fish" bowl, the less people really know about you![45]

January 7, 1936, "My Day"

I'm weary of cheering crowds. (I'd like them less if they booed but I'd be more interested!)[46]

June 11, 1936, letter to Lorena Hickok

How I hate being a show but I'm doing it *so* nicely.[47]

October 14, 1936, letter to Lorena Hickok, while on tour with FDR

Why can't someone have this job who'd like it & do something worth while with it?[48]

January 21, 1937, letter to Lorena Hickok

I could never say in the morning, "I have a headache and cannot do thus and so." Headache or no headache, thus and so had to be done.[49]

Circa 1937, *This Is My Story*

[N]o, I don't look forward to the next four years for I will probably be too old for a new job at the end & I dread getting accustomed to 4 more years of easy living but perhaps I can keep from being too dependent on it. Anyway what is the use of worrying about tomorrow let alone 4 years from now![50]

November 8, 1940, letter to Lorena Hickok, remarking on her continuing role as First Lady after the reelection of FDR

Always be on time. Never try to make any personal engagements. Do as little talking as humanly possible. Never be disturbed by anything. Always do what you're told to do as quickly as possible. Remember to lean back in a parade, so that people can see your husband. Don't get too fat to ride three on a seat. Get out of the way as quickly as you can when you are not needed.[51]

Circa 1940, advice to future First Ladies

Almost any woman in the White House during these years of need would have done what I have done—tried to help.[52]

January 25, 1941, *New York Times*

I have all the pomp & restriction & none of the power![53]

September 6, 1943, letter to Joseph P. Lash

For many years of my life I realized that what my husband was attempting to do was far more important than anything which I could possibly accomplish; and therefore I never said anything, or wrote anything, without first balancing it against the objectives which I thought he was working for at the time. We did not always agree as to methods, but our ultimate objectives were fortunately very much the same.[54]

July 9, 1946, *Look*

[N]ow, when I speak, no one will attribute my thoughts to someone holding an important office and whose work may be hurt and not helped thereby. If people do not like what I say nowadays, they can blame me, but it will hurt no one else's plans or policies.[55]

July 9, 1946, *Look*

I am an individual and so was my husband. It happens that on nearly all big issues we agreed but any two people are bound to differ now and then, on method if not on principle.[56]

Circa 1946, *If You Ask Me*, response to a question on if she and her husband
always agreed

I never urged on him a specific course of action, no matter how strongly I felt, because I realized he knew of factors in the picture as a whole of which I might be ignorant.[57]

Circa 1949, *This I Remember*

On the whole, however, I think I lived those years very impersonally. It was almost as thought I had erected someone a little outside myself who was the president's wife. I was lost somewhere deep down inside myself.[58]

Circa 1949, *This I Remember*, on her years as First Lady

I have spent many years of my life in opposition and I rather like the role.[59]

November 18, 1952, letter to Bernard Baruch

Do you think that if I stopped working for six months anyone would remember *me*?[60]

Circa September 1959

You will feel that you are no longer clothing yourself, you are dressing a public monument.[61]

October 27, 1960, *New York Herald Tribune*, comment to future First Wives about
their wardrobes

On Her Politics and Political Role

You need not be proud of me. . . . I'm only being *active* til you can be again—it isn't such a great desire on my part to serve the world and I'll fall back into habits of sloth quite easily![62]

February 5, 1924, letter to FDR, reassuring him that her role in politics was only temporary while he recovered from polio

I say what I believe, but I will not stump against my party regardless of its program.[63]

Circa 1932

I took an interest in politics, but I don't know whether I enjoyed it! It was a wife's duty to be interested in whatever interested her husband.[64]

Circa 1937, *This Is My Story*

People can gradually be brought to understand that an individual, even if she is a President's wife, may have independent views and must be allowed the expression of an opinion. But actual participation in the work of the Government, we are not yet able to accept.[65]

February 23, 1942, "My Day," reflecting on her brief term as the assistant national director for the Office of Civilian Defense

I feel I must tell you that nothing could induce me to run for any public office. I seriously doubt any woman could be nominated, but even in that eventuality, I could not even permit my name to be entered.[66]

June 13, 1947, *New York Times*

Though Franklin always said I was far too impatient ever to be a good politician, and though my sense of timing is nowhere near so trustworthy as his was, I have grown more patient with age and have learned from my husband that no leader can be too far ahead of his followers.[67]

Circa 1949, *This I Remember*

The truth is I don't like politics especially. I probably know too much about it—and the sacrifices it demands.[68]

October 10, 1954, *New York Times*

I know my satisfaction is not in politics, not in the interesting things I do. It is in being with people.[69]

Circa 1960, *You Learn by Living*

On Her Dealings with the Press

I will never be caught again that's sure and I'd like to crawl away for shame.[70]

July 24, 1917, letter to FDR, response to a humiliating *New York Times* article

If that story comes out about my nervous breakdown, I want you to send me a clipping, because it's a wonderful story. I haven't got the clipping, so I think perhaps he got cold feet.[71]

May 13, 1941, White House press conference, referring to the story of a journalist who threatened a false story of a nervous breakdown if she refused his interview

If I had the skill, I would write the saga of my own shortcomings as they are presented to me daily through the mail and the press. It would make amusing reading because of its variety and the many contradictions.[72]

August 20, 1943, "My Day"

On Her Security

Where would they hide us? They certainly couldn't cram us into the trunk of a car![73]

Summer of 1933, response to concerns about kidnapping threats while traveling with Lorena Hickok. (ER was nearly six feet tall, and Lorena weighed close to 250 pounds.)

On Assassination Attempts

One cannot live in fear.[74]

February 1933, response to an unsuccessful assassination attempt against FDR

If they want to get you, they can, and so the only thing you can do is just go along and not think about such things any more than you have to.[75]

February 17, 1933, *New York Times*

I'd step in front of him, of course.[76]

Circa 1933, on what she would do if someone attacked FDR

On Her Public Speaking

I do not think I shall ever get over being nervous before a speech, especially a speech for young people.[77]

June 9, 1936, "My Day"

I have a curiously artificial way of speaking, which annoys me terribly when I hear it afterwards.[78]

October 19, 1942, "My Day"

On Her Philosophy

If I have a philosophy, it would resolve itself into an effort not to make anybody suffer unnecessarily.[79]

November 17, 1936, *New York Times*

[T]o bring as little unhappiness to the world as possible.[80]

Circa 1946, *If You Ask Me*

Eleanor Roosevelt and Queen Elizabeth en route to the White House, June 8, 1939.
Courtesy of the Franklin D. Roosevelt Library and Museum.

17 ✳ Eleanor Roosevelt on Others

On the Roosevelt Family

They in all their serene assurance and absolute judgments on people and affairs going on in the world, make me want to squirm and turn Bolshevik.[1]

December 1920, letter to FDR

[T]he Delanos might disapprove of one another, and if so they were not slow to express their disapproval, but let someone so much as hint at criticism, and the clan was ready to tear him limb from limb![2]

Circa 1961, *The Autobiography of Eleanor Roosevelt*

On Anna Livingston Ludlow Hall, Her Mother

My mother was one of the most beautiful women I have ever seen.[3]

Circa 1937, *This Is My Story*

On Elliott Roosevelt, Her Father

He dominated my life as long as he lived, and was the love of my life for many years after he died.[4]

Circa 1937, *This Is My Story*

On Her Children

I determined that I would never be dependent on my children by allowing all my interests to center in them.[5]

Circa 1919

[They] regard me as a woman to be dutifully and affectionately thought of because I am their mother but . . . I hold queer opinions [that] can't be considered seriously against those of their usual male environment.[6]

Circa 1925–26, on her sons' attitude toward her opinions

Of course the thing I am proudest of is that I have produced five children, all of whom, I can say without reservation, are pretty nice people.[7]

October 8, 1944, *New York Times*

On Anna Roosevelt Dall Boettiger Halsted (1906–1975), Her Daughter

With my daughter I feel the bond that exists with any child, but, in addition, there has grown between us the deep understanding such as exists with an intimate friend.[8]

January 13, 1941, "My Day"

On Franklin Delano Roosevelt (1882–1945), Her Husband

If infantile paralysis didn't kill him, the Presidency won't.[9]

Circa 1932, response to concerns about FDR's health

From the personal standpoint, I did not want my husband to be president. I realized, however, that it was impossible to keep a man out of public service and that was what he wanted and was undoubtedly well equipped for. It was pure selfishness on my part, and I never mentioned my feelings on the subject to him.[10]

Circa 1961, *The Autobiography of Eleanor Roosevelt*

Dear I realize more & more that FDR is a great man & he is nice to me but as a person I'm a stranger & I don't want to be anything else.[11]

October 16, 1936, letter to Lorena Hickok

We've just come up from F's speech & I think it was good, if a bit arrogant in spots. He did not stir me but I may have been too tired or perhaps he can't.[12]

April 14, 1938, letter to Lorena Hickok, referring to FDR's "Fireside Chat"

No man who has brought himself back from what might have been an entire life of invalidism to physical, mental and spiritual strength and activity can ever be accused of preaching or exemplifying a mollycoddle philosophy.[13]

October 5, 1936, "My Day," response to criticism of her husband by her cousin Alice Roosevelt Longworth

Last night I had written questions & was asked if I loved my husband, which I did not answer![14]

September 23, 1939, letter to Lorena Hickok

Franklin's death ended a period in history & now in its wake those of us who laid in his shadow have to start again under our own momentum & wonder what we can achieve.[15]

April 19, 1945, letter to Lorena Hickok

Many people tell me that my husband's voice in their homes actually made them feel that they were part of his family.[16]

May 12, 1945, "My Day"

Always in Franklin there was evident a sense of humor, which could turn the most serious subject into an object of fun at times when he thought those around him needed a little break in the tension or perhaps a reminder that they were not so important as they thought; for one can reach a point where one's importance looms so great that one simply cannot carry the responsibility. That was at the bottom of many of the jokes that he sometimes aimed at himself, as well as others.[17]

Circa 1949, *This I Remember*

I have never known a man who gave one a greater sense of security. That was because I never heard him say there was a problem that he thought it was impossible for human beings to solve. He recognized the difficulties and often said that while he did not know the answer; that somewhere a man could be found who could give the answer.[18]

Circa 1949, *This I Remember*

If I liked his speech after he delivered it, I always said so; if for any reason I disapproved of it, I said nothing. But I never expected him to pay any attention to my ideas—he was much too good a speaker to need any advice from me.[19]

Circa 1949, *This I Remember*

The President doesn't discuss these things with me. Many people think that he does, but most often the first I know of some decision is when I see it in the papers.[20]

July 12, 1944, *New York Times,* on FDR's decision to accept a fourth-term nomination

On Jane Addams

Miss Addams served humanity so well she should never be forgotten. Anyone who knew her, will remember the inspiration of her presence, but her spirit went far beyond the individuals who knew her. It affected the thinking and living of people all over the world.[21]

September 4, 1941, "My Day"

On Marian Anderson

I have rarely heard a more beautiful and moving voice or a more finished artist.[22]

February 21, 1936, "My Day"

On George Washington Carver

[O]ne of the most impressive people I have ever known. He had a beautiful face, and a serenity and dignity which I have rarely seen equaled in any human being.[23]

November 9, 1945, "My Day"

On Carrie Chapman Catt

[S]he has been an inspiration to all of us and continues to be in these times, when many of us find ourselves obliged to face situations we had hoped were gone forever. Her courage, patience, humor and perennially young outlook, which bows to new conditions and adjusts to them, are perhaps the most helpful things to see in this most confusing world.[24]

May 19, 1941, "My Day"

Madame Chiang Kai-shek

[A] woman who, through her own personality and her own service, has achieved a place in the world, not merely as the wife of Generalissimo Chiang Kai-shek, but as a representative of her people.[25]

February 19, 1943, "My Day"

She is two different people. She could talk very convincingly about democracy and its aims and ideas and be perfectly charming, but she hasn't any idea how to live it.[26]

December 5, 1945, *Boston Post*

On Winston Churchill

One must admire a man who can trust the people of his country so completely that he can tell them stark naked, cruel truths unafraid. That quality of courage is a kind of challenge which calls to the very depth of other human souls.[27]

April 29, 1941, "My Day"

Winston Churchill, had besides the courage . . . the ability to put in words what his people felt so that he could always lead them.[28]

November 23, 1957, interview by Mike Wallace

On Marie Curie

One looks at this chic, well-groomed, delicate French woman and marvels at the calm with which she must have faced many danger-ous moments, and one is proud of women![29]

May 25, 1942, "My Day"

I imagine Mme. Curie will always be considered great, because she demonstrated that a woman's brain has as much ability for scientific research as a man's, and that a woman can be as steadfast in purpose and as self-denying in her work.[30]

Circa 1946, *If You Ask Me*

On Florence Nightingale

Florence Nightingale is one of the greatest women in history be-cause she contributed a new conception of one of the purposes to which women should dedicate themselves.[31]

Circa 1946, *If You Ask Me*

On Thomas Edison (1847–1931), Inventor

By his many inventions, Thomas Edison has probably changed our world more than any man of his time.[32]

February 11, 1944, "My Day"

On Albert Einstein (1879–1955), Theoretical Physicist

[S]o German & so simple with many wise gentle German qualities.[33]

January 24, 1934, letter to Lorena Hickok

On Dwight D. Eisenhower

It will be a sad day for him & in a way for the country, if he runs for President. He will run, but as a hero he will be tarnished & it will get worse & worse. We need our heroes & we need him here & I doubt if we need him more as President.[34]

January 21, 1945, letter to Joseph P. Lash

Lorena Hickok, Journalist and Friend

I've never enjoyed being with anyone the way I enjoy being with you.[35]

March 11, 1933, letter to Lorena Hickok

On Louis Howe, Political Advisor and Friend

He was like a pitiful, querulous child but even when I complained I loved him & no one will ever be more loyal & devoted than he was.[36]

April 19, 1936, letter to Lorena Hickok

On Missy LeHand, FDR's Private Secretary

If I should outlive F.D.R.[,] Missy would be the one I should worry about.[37]

April 19, 1936, letter to Lorena Hickok

On John F. Kennedy

I found him a brilliant man with a quick mind, anxious to learn, hospitable to new ideas, hardheaded in his approach. . . . He was not simply ambitious to be president; he wanted, I felt convinced to be a truly great president.[38]

Circa 1961, *The Autobiography of Eleanor Roosevelt*

On Richard Nixon

Mr. Nixon never has anything but hindsight.[39]

February 1, 1960, "My Day"

On Westbrook Pegler (1894–1969), Journalist and Critic

The poor man needs to be able to say disagreeable things.[40]

Circa November 1944

On Ernie Pyle (1900–1945), Journalist

I admired this frail and modest man who could endure hardships because he loved his job and our men.[41]

April 19, 1945, "My Day"

Harry S. Truman (1884–1972), American President

[H]e's the loneliest man I ever saw.[42]

Circa June 1945

Westbrook Pegler (*bottom left*), one of the First Lady's fiercest critics, and Eleanor Roosevelt laughing together in Pawling, New York, 1938. Courtesy of the Franklin D. Roosevelt Library and Museum.

18 ❋ Others on Eleanor Roosevelt

Anna Roosevelt Dall Boettiger Halsted (1906–1975), Her Daughter

Mother was forced into the position of disciplinarian. Mother did her duty.[1]

Circa 1962

J. Edgar Hoover (1895–1972), FBI Director

I often wonder whether she is so naïve as she professes or whether it is just a blind to lull the unsuspecting.[2]

Circa July 1950, notation from her FBI file

Fanny Hurst (1889–1968), Novelist

[T]he women of America are catching on to the fact that she is one of the greatest things that ever happened to them.[3]

March 1, 1935, *Democratic Digest*

Esther Everett Lape (1881–1981), Teacher, Writer, Suffragette

Eleanor felt that people did the best they could with the genes they inherited and the experiences life had given them, and she viewed the results with compassion.[4]

Date unknown

London News Chronicle

She has walked with kings, but never lost the common touch. Immersed in politics, she has never acquired the hard professionalism of the politician.[5]

October 25, 1948, *Time*

Alice Roosevelt Longworth (1884–1980), Her Cousin

She always wanted to discuss things like whether contentment was better than happiness and whether they conflicted with one another. Things like that, which I didn't give a damn about.[6]

Date unknown

Westbrook Pegler (1894–1969), Journalist

This woman is a political force of enormous ambitions. I believe she is a menace, unscrupulous as to truth, vain and cynical, all with a pretense of exaggerated kindness and human feeling which deceives millions of gullible persons.[7]

November 23, 1957, interview by Mike Wallace

Francis Perkins (1880–1965), U.S. Secretary of Labor

Her genius is the capacity to love the human race and to hear and understand the misery and wants and aspirations of the people.[8]

June 25, 1936, *New York Times*

Edith Carow Roosevelt (1861–1948), Her Aunt

She is very plain. Her mouth and teeth seem to have no future. But the ugly duckling may turn out to be a swan.[9]

Circa 1893

Franklin is nine-tenths mush and one-tenth Eleanor.[10]

Circa 1920

Franklin Delano Roosevelt (1882–1945), Her Husband

Never get into an argument with the Missus, you can't win. . . . You think you have her pinned down here . . . but she bobs up right away over there somewhere! No use—you can't win![11]

Circa 1940–45

Dear God, please make Eleanor a little tired.[12]

Date unknown

Franklin Delano Roosevelt Jr. (1914–1988), Politician and Her Son

I am her son, yet it is more than kinship that impels me to say she was the most remarkable woman of the twentieth century.[13]

Circa 1984

Sara Ann Delano Roosevelt (1854–1941), Her Mother-in-Law

Your mother only bore you.[14]

Unknown date, Sara's assertion that her role in ER's children's lives was more important than their mother's

Saturday Review of Literature

Greatest woman in the world.[15]

January 6, 1951, *Saturday Review of Literature*

Marie Souvestre (1830–1905), Feminist Educator and Teacher

As a pupil she is very satisfactory, but even that is of small account when you compare it with the perfect quality of her soul.[16]

February 18, 1901, letter to ER's grandmother

Arthur B. Spingarn (1878–1971), Civil Rights Leader

The American Negro had no truer friend.[17]
December 1962, *Crisis*

Adlai Stevenson II (1900–1965), Ambassador to the United Nations

Like so many others, I have lost more than a beloved friend. I have lost an inspiration. She would rather light a candle than curse the darkness, and her glow has warmed the world.[18]
November 8, 1962, *New York Times*

Time magazine

Eleanor Roosevelt has become, perhaps, the best-known woman in the world. Three years after her husband's death, she has reversed the usual lot of presidents' widows by gaining measurably in stature and prestige. She is a unique combination of Citizeness Fix-it and great lady.[19]
October 25, 1948, *Time* magazine

Harry Truman

I appreciated her. I named her First Lady of the World![20]
Circa November 1962

Arthur Vandenberg, Republican Senator

I've said a lot of mean things about Mrs. Roosevelt, but I want to tell you that I take them all back. She's a grand person and a great American citizen.[21]
Date unknown

Notes

Preface and Acknowledgments

1. Eleanor Roosevelt, "My Day," Oct 25, 1945. "My Day" newspaper columns were nationally syndicated and were sometimes published on different days in different publications. For the purposes of consistency, "My Day" columns are cited according to the Eleanor Roosevelt Papers Project and can be found at www.gwu.edu/~erpapers/myday/.
2. This book will use the initials "ER" for Eleanor Roosevelt and "FDR" for Franklin Delano Roosevelt.
3. *Academy*, Dec 1901, 610.
4. Cook, *Eleanor Roosevelt* 1: 491.
5. ER, *This I Remember*, 8.
6. Beasley, *Eleanor Roosevelt and the Media*, 149.

Chapter 1. On Government and Politics

1. Cook, 1: 381.
2. Smith, *FDR*, 231–32.
3. Goodwin, *No Ordinary Time*, 204.
4. Pederson, *The FDR Years*, 124.
5. Beasley, Shulman, and Beasley, *The Eleanor Roosevelt Encyclopedia*, 31.
6. Morsink, *The Universal Declaration of Human Rights*, 21–27.
7. ER, "My Day," Oct 23, 1942.
8. "Mrs. Roosevelt Says . . ." *Western Mail* (Perth, Australia), Oct 21, 1943.
9. ER, "My Day," Sep 7, 1945.
10. Ibid., Nov 8, 1945.

11. Cook, 1: 276.
12. Ibid., 1: 304.
13. ER, "My Day," Aug 9, 1938.
14. ER, *The White House Press Conferences*, 72.
15. ER, "My Day," Jul 1, 1940.
16. Ibid., Jun 13, 1944.
17. Ibid., Nov 8, 1944.
18. Ibid., Jul 2, 1945.
19. Ibid., Feb 13, 1957.
20. ER, *You Learn by Living*, 171.
21. ER, *The White House Press Conferences*, 77.
22. ER, *This I Remember*, 63.
23. ER, *You Learn by Living*, 197.
24. Ibid., 203.
25. ER, *Tomorrow Is Now*, 124–25.
26. ER and Hickok, *Empty without You*, 187–88.
27. ER, *The Autobiography of Eleanor Roosevelt*, 425.
28. Ibid., 426.
29. ER, "My Day," Jan 7, 1941.
30. Lash, *A World of Love*, 131.
31. ER, "Why I Do Not Choose to Run," *Look*, Jul 9, 1946.
32. James MacGregor Burns and Janet Thompson Burns, "Mrs. Roosevelt a Remarkable 75," *NYT*, Oct 4, 1959.
33. ER, *The Autobiography of Eleanor Roosevelt*, 421.
34. ER Papers Project, www.gwu.edu/%7Eerpapers/documents/correspondence/doc005370b.cfm.
35. ER, "Why I Do Not Choose to Run," *Look*, Jul 9, 1946.
36. ER, *If You Ask Me*, 55.
37. Ibid., 59.
38. "Two Scrappy 75-Year-Old Democrats," *Life*, Dec 21, 1959, 35.
39. ER and Hickok, 188.
40. Ibid., 233.
41. ER, "My Day," May 29, 1941.
42. Roosevelt and Brough, *Mother R*, 26.
43. Lash, *A World of Love*, 189.
44. ER and Truman, *Eleanor and Harry*, 37.
45. Ibid., 63.
46. ER, "My Day," Aug 21, 1936.

47. "Mrs. F. D. Roosevelt Tells Marshall Seniors That Intellectual Peaks Must Stand," *NYT*, Jun 17, 1937.

48. Lash, *Eleanor and Franklin*, 768.

49. ER, *The White House Press Conferences*, 112.

50. ER, "Keepers of Democracy," *Virginia Quarterly Review*, Jan 1939, 4.

51. ER, "Insuring Democracy," *Collier's*, Jun 15, 1940, 87.

52. ER, "The Moral Basis of Democracy," in ER, *Courage in a Dangerous World*, 50.

53. Ibid., 56.

54. ER, "My Day," Sep 30, 1941.

55. Ibid., May 26, 1943.

56. "Mrs. Roosevelt Lives Up to Reputation," *Argus* (Melbourne, Australia), Sep 6, 1943.

57. "Mrs. Roosevelt Says . . ." *Western Mail* (Perth, Australia), Oct 21, 1943.

58. ER, *India and the Awakening East*, 227.

59. Ibid., 228.

60. ER and Truman, 245.

61. ER, *The Autobiography of Eleanor Roosevelt*, 401. Also in ER, "What Has Happened to the American Dream?," *Atlantic Monthly*, Apr 1961, 47.

62. ER, *The Autobiography of Eleanor Roosevelt*, 401.

63. ER, *Tomorrow Is Now*, 45.

64. Ibid., 119–20.

65. Ibid., 125.

66. Lash, *A World of Love*, 63.

67. Wotkyns, *With Love, Aunt Eleanor*, 82.

68. ER, "My Day," Jan 25, 1940.

69. Ibid., Jun 9, 1945.

70. Ibid., Feb 12, 1947.

71. ER, *The Eleanor Roosevelt Papers*, 1: 937.

72. ER, "If You Ask Me," *McCall's Magazine*, Sep 1953, 16. ER wrote the monthly column, "If You Ask Me," for *Ladies' Home Journal* (May 1941–1949) and *McCall's Magazine* (1949–1962).

73. ER, "My Day," Mar 21, 1936.

74. ER, "If You Ask Me," *McCall's Magazine*, Feb 1950, 28.

75. ER, "My Day," Mar 23, 1942.

76. ER, *Eleanor Roosevelt's Book of Common Sense Etiquette*, 550.

77. Ibid.

78. ER, "My Day," Jan 21, 1941.

79. "First Lady Backs Leviton Strikers," *NYT*, Feb 6, 1941.

80. ER, "My Day," Jul 11, 1942.

81. Ibid., Aug 24, 1943.

82. Ibid., Jun 22, 1944.

83. Ibid., Jul 22, 1944.

84. ER, "Why I Do Not Choose to Run," *Look*, Jul 9, 1946.

85. ER, *You Learn by Living*, 189.

86. ER, *The Autobiography of Eleanor Roosevelt*, 402.

87. ER, *Tomorrow Is Now*, 89.

88. ER, "My Day," May 31, 1937.

89. Ibid., Dec 3, 1943.

90. Wotkyns, 124.

91. ER, "My Day," Nov 15, 1940.

92. Ibid., Nov 3, 1943.

93. Ibid.

94. ER, "Old Age Pensions," in ER, *Courage in a Dangerous World*, 20.

95. ER, "My Day," Mar 2, 1943.

96. Ibid., Aug 24, 1945.

97. Ibid., October 6, 1945.

98. ER and Truman, 104.

99. ER, "Liberals in This Year of Decision," *Christian Register*, Jun 1948, 26.

100. ER, "What Has Happened to the American Dream?," *Atlantic Monthly*, Apr 1961, 47.

101. ER, *The Autobiography of Eleanor Roosevelt*, 415.

102. ER, *Tomorrow Is Now*, 45.

103. ER, "My Day," Jan 29, 1948.

104. ER and Truman, 217.

105. "Mrs. Roosevelt Given Rousing Ovation at Convention," *Wallingford (Conn.) Meriden Daily Journal*, Jul 23, 1952.

106. ER, *India and the Awakening East*, 229.

107. ER, *The Autobiography of Eleanor Roosevelt*, 433.

Chapter 2. On Nations

1. The Eleanor Roosevelt Papers Project provides excellent details of her travels over the years: www.gwu.edu/~erpapers/maps/main_map.html.

2. ER, "My Day," Jun 30, 1942.

3. ER, *The Eleanor Roosevelt Papers*, 1: 140.

4. ER, *If You Ask Me*, 63.

5. "Mrs. Roosevelt Hits Mme. Chiang: Says She Could Talk about Democracy but Didn't Know How to Live it," *Boston Post*, Dec 5, 1945.

6. ER, "My Day," Sep 2, 1944.

7. Ibid., Dec 3, 1948.

8. ER, *You Learn by Living*, 20.

9. ER, *The Eleanor Roosevelt Papers*, 1: 72.

10. ER, "My Day," Oct 13, 1945.

11. ER, *India and the Awakening East*, 134.

12. Ibid., 171.

13. Lash, *Eleanor: The Years Alone*, 115.

14. S. J. Woolf, "The New Chapter in Mrs. Roosevelt's Life," *NYT Magazine*, Dec 15, 1946.

15. ER, "My Day," Feb 20, 1952. Similar quote: ER, *The Autobiography of Eleanor Roosevelt*, 402.

16. ER, "My Day," Apr 30, 1958.

17. Lash, *A World of Love*, 32.

18. ER, "My Day," Jun 1, 1945.

19. ER, *The Eleanor Roosevelt Papers*, 1: 187.

20. "Russians Weighed by Mrs. Roosevelt," *NYT*, Feb 16, 1946.

21. ER, *The Eleanor Roosevelt Papers*, 1: 974.

22. ER, *The Autobiography of Eleanor Roosevelt*, 391–92.

23. Ibid., 394.

24. Ibid., 397.

25. "Job Hints Offered by Mrs. Roosevelt," *NYT*, Jun 28, 1940.

26. ER, "My Day," Jan 6, 1941.

27. ER, "Social Gains and Defense," in ER, *Courage in a Dangerous World*, 135.

28. ER, "My Day," Sep 23, 1941.

29. ER and A. Roosevelt, *Mother & Daughter*, 156–57.

30. ER, "My Day," Mar 8, 1943.

31. Ibid., Oct 9, 1943.

32. Lash, *A World of Love*, 75.

33. ER, "My Day," Feb 26, 1944.

34. Ibid., Apr 17, 1944.

35. Ibid., Sep 28, 1945.

36. ER and Truman, 46.

37. ER, *The Eleanor Roosevelt Papers*, 1: 733.

38. ER, "My Day," May 18, 1949.

39. Wotkyns, 112.

40. Ibid., 129.

41. ER, *India and the Awakening East*, 114.

42. Wotkyns, 110.

43. ER, "My Day," Feb 27, 1961.

44. ER, *Tomorrow Is Now*, 17.

45. ER, *The Autobiography of Eleanor Roosevelt*, 408.

46. Ibid., 409.

Chapter 3. On History, War, and Peace

1. Eunice Fuller Barnard, "Mrs. Roosevelt in the Classroom," *NYT Magazine*, Dec 4, 1932.

2. ER, *The Autobiography of Eleanor Roosevelt*, 91–93.

3. ER, "My Day," Jul 27, 1942.

4. Goodwin, 465.

5. Beasley, 278.

6. ER, *It's Up to the Women*, 158. Similar quote: Catt, et al., *Why Wars Must Cease*, 27.

7. ER, *The White House Press Conferences*, 88.

8. ER, "My Day," Oct 23, 1942.

9. Ibid., Feb 13, 1943.

10. Ibid., Jul 31, 1943.

11. Ibid.

12. ER, "Keynote Address to the New York Democratic State Convention," Sep 3, 1946, ER Papers Project, www.gwu.edu/~erpapers/documents/displaydoc.cfm?_t=speeches&_docid=spc026185.

13. ER, *You Learn by Living*, 16–17.

14. ER, *The Autobiography of Eleanor Roosevelt*, 409.

15. ER, *Tomorrow Is Now*, xvi.

16. Ibid., 4.

17. Lash, *Eleanor and Franklin*, 285.

18. "Mrs. F. D. Roosevelt a Civic Worker," *NYT*, Nov 9, 1932.

19. Black, *Eleanor Roosevelt*, 161.

20. ER, *If You Ask Me*, 80.

21. ER, "I Want You to Write to Me," *Woman's Home Companion*, Aug 1933, 4.

22. ER, "My Day," Nov 26, 1943.

23. Kearney, *Anna Eleanor Roosevelt*, 49.

24. ER, "Why I Still Believe in the Youth Congress," *Liberty*, Apr 20, 1940, 31.

25. ER, "My Day," Oct 29, 1947.

26. Ibid.

27. Ibid., Aug 29, 1952.

28. ER, "Because the War Idea Is Obsolete," in ER, *Courage in a Dangerous World*, 84. Similar quote: ER, *The White House Press Conferences*, 48.

29. ER, *Courage in a Dangerous World*, 85.

30. ER, "My Day," Feb 28, 1936.

31. Ibid., Mar 13, 1936.

32. Ibid., Mar 18, 1936.

33. Ibid., Feb 7, 1939.

34. ER, "Civil Liberties--The Individual and the Community," address to the Chicago Civil Liberties Committee, Mar 14, 1940, *Reference Shelf*, 1940.

35. ER, "My Day," Mar 12, 1942.

36. ER, "Must We Hate to Fight?," *Saturday Review of Literature*, Jul 4, 1942, 13. Similar quote: ER, "My Day," Jul 10, 1942.

37. ER, "My Day," Aug 27, 1942.

38. Ibid., Mar 8, 1943.

39. Ibid., Apr 20, 1943.

40. Ibid., Jun 19, 1943.

41. "International Unity Plea by Mrs. Roosevelt," *Morning Bulletin* (Rockhampton, Queensland, Australia), Sep 6, 1943. Similar quote: "Mrs. Roosevelt Says . . . ," *Western Mail* (Perth, Australia), Oct 21, 1943.

42. ER, "My Day," Mar 6, 1944.

43. Ibid., Apr 10, 1944.

44. Ibid., Aug 16, 1944.

45. Ibid., Jun 5, 1945.

46. ER, *If You Ask Me*, 100.

47. ER and Truman, 133.

48. ER, *This I Remember*, 292.

49. Ibid., 60.

50. ER, "My Day," Oct 5, 1957.

51. ER and A. Roosevelt, 105–6.

52. ER and Hickok, 240.

53. ER, "My Day," Jan 3, 1942.

54. Ibid., Feb 17, 1942.

55. Ibid., Mar 10, 1942.

56. ER and Hickok, 245

57. Ibid., 247.

58. ER, "My Day," Dec 5, 1942.

59. Ibid., Jan 23, 1943.

60. ER and Hickok, 250–51.

61. ER, "My Day," Oct 5, 1943.

62. Ibid., Oct 28, 1943.

63. Ibid., Feb 9, 1944.

64. Ibid., Jun 7, 1944.

65. Ibid., Aug 26, 1944.

66. Ibid., Nov 21, 1944.

67. Ibid., May 9, 1945.

68. Ibid.

69. Ibid., Aug 15, 1945.

70. Ibid., Aug 18, 1945.

71. Ibid., Sep 25, 1942.

72. Ibid., Apr 30, 1945.

73. Ibid., Sep 5, 1945.

74. Ibid., May 23, 1941.

75. Ibid., Jul 11, 1942.

76. Ibid., Sep 1, 1942.

77. Ibid., Oct 15, 1943.

78. Lash, *A World of Love*, 126.

79. ER, "My Day," Aug 8, 1945.

80. Ibid., Aug 15, 1945.

81. Ibid., Aug 27, 1945.

82. Ibid., Sep 5, 1945.

83. Ibid., Sep 25, 1945.

84. Ibid.

85. Ibid.

86. Ibid., Oct 3, 1945.
87. ER, *The Eleanor Roosevelt Papers*, 1: 182; and also "Her UNO Task Set by Mrs. Roosevelt," *NYT*, Jan 6, 1946.
88. ER, "My Day," Apr 16, 1954.
89. ER, *This I Remember*, 112.
90. ER, "My Day," Jan 28, 1942.
91. Ibid., Nov 6, 1942.
92. Ibid., Jul 30, 1943.
93. Ibid., Jun 17, 1944.
94. Ibid., Oct 29, 1945.
95. Ibid., Sep 2, 1947.
96. "Aliens Reassured by Mrs. Roosevelt," *NYT*, Apr 7, 1942.
97. ER, "My Day," Oct 25, 1941.
98. Ibid., Jun 12, 1942.
99. Ibid., May 14, 1943.
100. The original text refers to "the martyrdom of the Jews in Warsaw."
101. ER, "My Day," Jun 8, 1944.
102. Ibid., Apr 28, 1945.
103. Ibid., May 2, 1945.
104. Ibid., Sep 24, 1945.
105. Ibid., May 9, 1945.
106. Ibid., Aug 16, 1945.
107. ER and Truman, 59.
108. ER, "My Day," Aug 11, 1945.
109. ER, "This Troubled World," in ER, *Courage in a Dangerous World*, 92.
110. Ibid., 100.
111. ER, "My Day," Aug 26, 1939.
112. ER, *The White House Press Conferences*, 133.
113. ER, "My Day," Dec 9, 1942.
114. Ibid., Dec 16, 1943.
115. Ibid., Jan 7, 1944.
116. Ibid., Sep 13, 1944.
117. Ibid., Oct 6, 1945. Similar quote: ER, "My Day," Aug 18, 1945.
118. Ibid., Oct 12, 1945.
119. ER, *The Eleanor Roosevelt Papers*, 1: 137.
120. ER, *If You Ask Me*, 143.
121. ER, "My Day," Aug 30, 1947.

122. ER, "Liberals in This Year of Decision," *Christian Register*, Jun 1948, 33.

123. Voice of America broadcast, Nov 11, 1951.

124. ER and Truman, 217.

125. ER, "My Day," Jan 22, 1959.

Chapter 4. On Religion

1. ER, *This I Remember*, 44–45.

2. Ibid., 116.

3. ER, *Courage in a Dangerous World*, 253–54.

4. ER, "What Religion Means to Me," *Forum*, Dec 1932, 324.

5. ER, "My Day," Jul 14, 1943.

6. Lash, *A World of Love*, 83.

7. ER, "The Moral Basis of Democracy," in ER, *Courage in a Dangerous World*, 53.

8. ER, "My Day," Jan 2, 1941.

9. Ibid., Apr 15, 1941.

10. Ibid., Oct 10, 1941.

11. ER, "If You Ask Me," *Ladies' Home Journal*, Oct 1941, 133.

12. ER, "My Day," Sept 23, 1943.

13. Lash, *A World of Love*, 121.

14. ER, "My Day," Nov 25, 1944.

15. Ibid., Dec 25, 1944.

16. Ibid., May 7, 1945.

17. Ibid., Aug 8, 1946.

18. ER, *If You Ask Me*, 82. Similar quote: ER, "If You Ask Me," *McCall's Magazine*, Aug 1954.

19. ER, *If You Ask Me*, 123.

20. ER, "My Day," Dec 10, 1948.

21. ER, *Courage in a Dangerous World*, 259.

22. ER, "My Day," Sep 27, 1950.

23. ER, "If You Ask Me," *McCall's Magazine*, Sep 1953, 16.

24. Ibid., Aug 1954.

25. ER, "My Day," Sep 13, 1947.

26. ER, *India and the Awakening East*, 24.

27. ER, "My Day," Sep 20, 1960.

28. ER, *The Autobiography of Eleanor Roosevelt*, 438.

29. ER, *The White House Press Conferences*, 146.

30. ER, "My Day," Jul 15, 1949.

31. ER, *Courage in a Dangerous World*, 257.

32. Ibid., 258.
33. ER, "My Day," Jun 23, 1949.
34. ER, *It Seems to Me*, 172.
35. ER, "My Day," Apr 22, 1936.
36. Ibid., Nov 22, 1944.
37. Ibid., Apr 26, 1945.
38. Ibid., Apr 14, 1953.
39. Lash, *Eleanor: The Years Alone*, 302.
40. ER, *You Learn by Living*, 85–86.
41. Wotkyns, 24. Similar quote: Wotkyns, 58–59.

Chapter 5. On Freedoms, Rights, and Threats to Them

1. ER, *Courage in a Dangerous World*, 150.
2. ER, "Civil Liberties—The Individual and the Community," address to the Chicago Civil Liberties Committee, Mar 14, 1940, in ER, *Courage in a Dangerous World*, 130.
3. Glendon, *A World Made New*, 301.
4. Statements at presentation of *In Your Hands: A Guide for Community Action for the Tenth Anniversary of the Universal Declaration of Human Rights*, http://www.udhr.org/history/inyour.htm.
5. ER and Hickok, 37.
6. ER, *The Autobiography of Eleanor Roosevelt*, 426.
7. Ibid., 427.
8. ER, "My Day," Apr 15, 1943.
9. Ibid., May 11, 1943.
10. ER, "A Challenge to American Sportsmanship," *Collier's*, Oct 16, 1943, 71.
11. ER, "My Day," May 30, 1944.
12. Ibid., Oct 20, 1944.
13. Ibid., Nov 2, 1945.
14. ER, *If You Ask Me*, 117.
15. Ibid., 131.
16. ER, *The Eleanor Roosevelt Papers*, 1: 644.
17. ER, "My Day," Sep 3, 1949.
18. ER, "Reply to Attacks on U.S. Attitude toward Human Rights Covenant," *Department of State Bulletin*, Jan 14, 1952, 59.
19. Interview by Mike Wallace, Nov 23, 1957, www.hrc.utexas.edu/multimedia/video/2008/wallace/roosevelt_eleanor.html.

20. ER, *You Learn by Living*, 152.

21. ER, *The Autobiography of Eleanor Roosevelt*, 398.

22. ER, "My Day," Oct 29, 1947.

23. Ibid., May 11, 1943.

Chapter 6. On Work

1. ER, *The Autobiography of Eleanor Roosevelt*, 154.

2. ER, "Building Character," *Parent's Magazine*, Jun 1931, 17.

3. ER, *The White House Press Conferences*, 14.

4. "Mrs. Franklin D. Roosevelt's Page," *Woman's Home Companion*, Nov 1933, 4. Similar quote: ER, "My Day," Jun 16, 1939.

5. ER, "My Day," Apr 21, 1938.

6. Ibid., Mar 14, 1941.

7. Ibid., Sept 1, 1941.

8. Ibid., Aug 7, 1941.

9. Ibid., Oct 1, 1942.

10. Mackenzie, *Mr. Roosevelt*, 102.

11. ER, *On My Own*, 7. Similar quote: ER, "My Day," Jul 3, 1943.

12. ER, *You Learn by Living*, 55.

13. ER, *Tomorrow Is Now*, 45.

14. Lash, *Eleanor and Franklin*, 238.

15. ER, "My Day," Mar 29, 1941.

16. ER, *If You Ask Me*, 78.

17. Ibid., 122.

18. ER, "My Day," Oct 17, 1955.

19. "Mrs. Roosevelt Tells of Woman-Run Factory," *NYT*, Nov 16, 1930.

20. ER, *It's Up to the Women*, 150.

21. Susan B. Anthony II, "Woman's Next Step," *NYT*, Jan 12, 1941.

22. ER, "My Day," Apr 19, 1943.

23. Ibid., Oct 22, 1943.

24. ER, *If You Ask Me*, 119.

25. ER, "My Day," Apr 29, 1936.

26. Ibid.

27. ER, "My Day," Feb 20, 1936.

28. Ibid., Sep 20, 1945.

29. Ibid., Mar 13, 1941.

30. Ibid.

31. Ibid., Apr 16, 1943.
32. ER, *If You Ask Me*, 149.
33. ER, "My Day," Aug 22, 1952.
34. Farr, 164.
35. "First Lady Asks Miners to Halt Strike in Crisis," *NYT*, Apr 30, 1943. Similar quote: ER, "My Day," May 1, 1943.
36. ER, "My Day," Jun 6, 1944.
37. ER, *If You Ask Me*, 106.
38. ER, *You Learn by Living*, 200–201.

Chapter 7. On Money and Economics

1. ER, *This Is My Story*, 96.
2. ER, "My Day," Aug 15, 1936.
3. ER, *If You Ask Me*, 79.
4. ER, "My Day," Jan 27, 1953.
5. ER, *You Learn by Living*, 157.
6. ER, "The State's Responsibility for Fair Working Conditions," *Scribner's Magazine*, Mar 1933, 140.
7. ER, "My Day," Jan 6, 1941.
8. Ibid., Oct 7, 1941.
9. Ibid., Nov 7, 1941.
10. Ibid., Jan 9, 1942.
11. Ibid., Jul 17, 1942.
12. Ibid., Nov 17, 1943.
13. Ibid., Jul 19, 1944.
14. "Mrs. Roosevelt Gets Degree in Ontario," *NYT*, Jan 9, 1948.
15. ER, "My Day," Feb 15, 1949.
16. Ibid., Mar 19, 1936.
17. Ibid., Aug 1, 1945.
18. Ibid., Apr 22, 1949.
19. ER, *Tomorrow Is Now*, 36.
20. Ibid., 43.
21. Interview by Mike Wallace, Nov 23, 1957, www.hrc.utexas.edu/multimedia/video/2008/wallace/roosevelt_eleanor.html.
22. ER, *Courage in a Dangerous World*, 261.
23. ER, "My Day," Feb 20, 1936.

Chapter 8. On Arts, Literature, and Leisure

1. ER, "My Day," Sep 4, 1941, Apr 23, 1942, Jul 21, 1954, and Nov 19, 1951.
2. Cook, 2: 162–63.
3. ER, *You Learn by Living*, 129, 96, and 152.
4. ER, "The New Governmental Interest in Arts," in ER, *Courage in a Dangerous World*, 27.
5. ER, *If You Ask Me*, 41.
6. ER, "My Day," Oct 17, 1944.
7. Ibid., Nov 5, 1958.
8. "The Press: Just Babies," *Time*, Jul 25, 1932.
9. ER, *This Is My Story*, 268.
10. Ibid., 358.
11. ER, "My Day," Apr 8, 1941.
12. Ibid., Jul 6, 1945.
13. Ibid., Nov 15, 1954.
14. ER, *You Learn by Living*, 7.
15. ER, *Tomorrow Is Now*, 72.
16. ER, "My Day," Apr 17, 1961.
17. ER, *Tomorrow Is Now*, 72.
18. ER, *The White House Press Conferences*, 10.
19. ER, "My Day," Jul 23, 1943.
20. Ibid., Mar 4, 1944.
21. Ibid., May 21, 1936.
22. Ibid., Oct 29, 1947.

Chapter 9. On Education and Learning

1. Lash, *Eleanor and Franklin*, 87.
2. Eunice Fuller Barnard, "Mrs. Roosevelt in the Classroom," *NYT Magazine*, Dec 4, 1932.
3. Cook, 1: 401.
4. ER, "The Ideal Education," *Woman's Journal*, Oct 1930, 9.
5. "Mrs. Roosevelt of the Strenuous Life," *NYT*, Oct 11, 1931.
6. Eunice Fuller Barnard, "Mrs. Roosevelt in the Classroom," *NYT Magazine*, Dec 4, 1932.
7. Ibid.

8. ER, "Are We Overlooking the Pursuit of Happiness?," *Parent's Magazine*, Sep 1936, 67.

9. "First Lady Chides Older Generation," *NYT*, Oct 19, 1937.

10. ER, "My Day," Mar 19, 1941.

11. ER, *If You Ask Me*, 29.

12. Ibid., 39.

13. ER, "My Day," Jan 12, 1942.

14. Ibid., Apr 20, 1942.

15. Ibid., Dec 30, 1942.

16. Ibid.

17. Ibid., Feb 11, 1943.

18. Ibid., May 11, 1943.

19. Ibid., Jan 24, 1944.

20. Ibid., Nov 3, 1945.

21. Ibid., Dec 22, 1945.

22. ER, *If You Ask Me*, 78.

23. ER, *This I Remember*, 132.

24. ER, "My Day," Feb 22, 1951.

25. ER, *You Learn by Living*, xii.

26. Ibid., xii.

27. Ibid., 14.

28. Ibid., 16.

29. Ibid., 130.

30. Ibid., 6.

31. Ibid., 4.

32. Ibid., 17.

33. Ibid., 14.

34. Ibid., 8.

35. Ibid., 16.

36. ER, "My Day," Apr 17, 1961.

37. ER, *Tomorrow Is Now*, 134.

38. ER, "Ten Rules for Success in Marriage," *Pictorial Review*, Dec 1931, 36.

39. ER, "My Day," Dec 17, 1942.

40. Ibid., Feb 8, 1936.

41. Ibid., Apr 19, 1943.

42. Ibid., Jan 24, 1944.

43. Ibid., May 21, 1957.

44. ER, *If You Ask Me*, 152.
45. ER, *On My Own*, 386.

Chapter 10. On Gender, Age, and Class

1. ER, *This Is My Story*, 139.
2. ER, *The White House Press Conferences*, 7.
3. ER, *If You Ask Me*, 61.
4. Lash, *Eleanor and Franklin*, 111.
5. Beasley, 209.
6. ER and Hickok, 111.
7. Beasley, 82.
8. ER, "My Day," Aug 7, 1936.
9. ER, "In Defense of Curiosity," *Saturday Evening Post*, Aug 24, 1935, 9.
10. ER, "Women in Politics," *Good Housekeeping*, Mar 1940, 68.
11. Ibid., Apr 1940, 45.
12. Ibid., 203.
13. ER, "My Day," Aug 7, 1941.
14. "Eleanor Roosevelt—Things She Has Said," *Australian Women's Weekly*, Sep 11, 1943.
15. ER, "My Day," Aug 25, 1945.
16. Ibid., Oct 9, 1945.
17. Ibid., Nov 29, 1945.
18. Lash, *A World of Love*, 221.
19. ER, *You Learn by Living*, 56.
20. Ibid., 77.
21. ER, *This Is My Story*, 139.
22. ER, *The White House Press Conferences*, 330.
23. ER, "My Day," Feb 23, 1945.
24. Ibid., May 14, 1945.
25. "Smith for President Will Be Demanded by State Convention," *NYT*, Apr 15, 1924. *Note*: Other sources cite this article as "Women Are in Revolt," which is one of four subtitles for the article.
26. Rose Feld, "Women Are Slow to Use the Ballot," *NYT*, Apr 20, 1924.
27. Ibid.
28. Ibid.
29. S. J. Woolf, "A Woman Speaks Her Political Mind," *NYT*, Apr 8, 1928.

30. ER, "Women Must Learn to Play the Game as Men Do," *Red Book Magazine*, Apr 1928, 79.

31. Ibid.

32. Ibid., 141.

33. ER, "Wives of Great Men," in ER, *What I Hope to Leave Behind*, 217.

34. ER, "Can a Woman Ever Be President of the United States?," *Cosmopolitan*, Oct 1935, 22. Similar quote: "Sees a Woman President," *NYT*, Jun 17, 1937.

35. ER, "My Day," Feb 3, 1936.

36. Cook, 2: 66.

37. ER, *The White House Press Conferences*, 66.

38. ER, "Women in Politics," *Good Housekeeping*, Mar 1940, 45.

39. ER, "My Day," May 19, 1941.

40. Ibid., Dec 10, 1942.

41. "Mrs. Roosevelt Says . . ." *Western Mail* (Perth, Australia), Oct 21, 1943.

42. ER, "Why I Do Not Choose to Run," *Look*, Jul 9, 1946.

43. ER, *If You Ask Me*, 102.

44. ER, "Wives of Great Men," in ER, *What I Hope to Leave Behind*, 217.

45. ER, "My Day," Mar 6, 1937.

46. ER, *This I Remember*, 292.

47. ER and Hickok, 229.

48. ER, "My Day," Aug 21, 1943.

49. Lash, *A World of Love*, 107.

50. Ibid., 109.

51. ER, "My Day," Sep 25, 1944.

52. Ibid., Oct 12, 1944.

53. Ibid., Feb 13, 1946.

54. Ibid., Jul 13, 1951.

55. ER, "Women Must Learn to Play the Game as Men Do," *Red Book Magazine*, Apr 1928, 79.

56. Ibid., 141.

57. "First Lady Urges Women 'to Count,'" *NYT*, Nov 4, 1943.

58. ER, "In Defense of Curiosity," *Saturday Evening Post*, Aug 24, 1935, 64.

59. ER, "My Day," Jul 16, 1936.

60. ER, "Insuring Democracy," *Collier's*, Jun 15, 1940, 87.

61. Ibid.

62. Ibid., 88.
63. ER, "My Day," Jun 26, 1943.
64. ER, "I Want You to Write to Me," *Woman's Home Companion*, Aug 1933, 4.
65. Lash, *Eleanor and Franklin*, 536.
66. ER, "My Day," Feb 18, 1936.
67. ER, "Why I Still Believe in the Youth Congress," *Liberty*, Apr 20, 1940.
68. ER, "My Day," Sep 4, 1942.
69. Ibid., Dec 14, 1942.
70. Ibid., Oct 5, 1945.
71. Ibid., Jun 29, 1951.
72. Hickok, *Reluctant First Lady*, 44.
73. "Mrs. Roosevelt 50 Today," *NYT*, Oct 11, 1934.
74. ER, "My Day," Apr 3, 1942.
75. Ibid., Sep 17, 1942.
76. Ibid., Oct 13, 1942.
77. Ibid., Oct 16, 1943.
78. ER, *This I Remember*, 148.
79. ER, "If You Ask Me," *McCall's Magazine*, Oct 1953. Also in ER, *You Learn by Living*, 63.
80. United States Congress, *Old Age Pensions, Hearings before the Committee on the District of Columbia, House of Representatives . . .*, 1934, 27.
81. ER, "My Day," Nov 9, 1938.
82. ER, *You Learn by Living*, 90.
83. Ibid., 68.
84. ER, *Eleanor Roosevelt's Book of Common Sense Etiquette*, 61.
85. ER, "Building Character," *Parent's Magazine*, Jun 1931, 17.
86. ER, *This Is My Story*, 362.
87. ER and Hickok, 232.
88. Lash, *A World of Love*, 30.
89. "Eleanor Roosevelt—Things She Has Said," *Australian Women's Weekly*, Sep 11, 1943.

Chapter 11. On Race and Ethnicity

1. Cook, 1: 317.
2. Black, *Casting Her Own Shadow*, 240.
3. ER, "In Defense of Curiosity," *Saturday Evening Post*, Aug 24, 1935, 66.
4. ER, *Courage in a Dangerous World*, 41.
5. ER, *The White House Press Conferences*, 198–99.
6. ER, "Intolerance," *Cosmopolitan*, Feb 1940, 102.
7. ER, "Race, Religion and Prejudice," *New Republic*, May 11, 1942, 630.
8. ER, "My Day," May 26, 1942.
9. Ibid., Jun 19, 1943.
10. Ibid., Nov 24, 1943.
11. ER, "Tolerance Is an Ugly Word," *Coronet*, Jul 1945, 118.
12. ER, *Courage in a Dangerous World*, 258.
13. ER, *You Learn by Living*, 144.
14. ER, *Tomorrow Is Now*, 59.
15. ER, "Keepers of Democracy," *Virginia Quarterly Review*, Jan 1939, 3.
16. Ibid., 4.
17. ER, "Intolerance," *Cosmopolitan*, Feb 1940, 24.
18. Ibid., 25.
19. Kearney, 70.
20. ER, "My Day," Feb 27, 1939.
21. ER, "Keepers of Democracy," *Virginia Quarterly Review*, Jan 1939, 4.
22. ER, "My Day," Sep 18, 1941.
23. Ibid., Dec 16, 1941.
24. Ibid., Apr 3, 1942.
25. ER, "Race, Religion and Prejudice," *New Republic*, May 11, 1942, 630.
26. ER, "My Day," May 19, 1943.
27. Ibid., Dec 16, 1944.
28. Ibid., Jul 17, 1945.
29. ER, *If You Ask Me*, 75.
30. Ibid., 129.
31. ER, *The Eleanor Roosevelt Papers*, 1: 976.
32. ER, *You Learn by Living*, 186.
33. ER, *Tomorrow Is Now*, 61.
34. ER, "My Day," Oct 3, 1960.
35. Lash, *Eleanor and Franklin*, 214.

36. Ibid., 577, citing ER, "Mrs. Roosevelt Answers Mr. Wells on the Future of the Jews," *Liberty*, Dec 31, 1938.

37. ER, "My Day," Aug 13, 1943.

38. ER, *If You Ask Me*, 58.

39. ER, "My Day," May 13, 1960.

40. ER, "Race, Religion and Prejudice," *New Republic*, May 11, 1942, 630.

41. Francis, *The Tuskegee Airmen*, 465.

42. ER, "If I Were a Negro," *Negro Digest*, Oct 1943, 8.

43. ER, "My Day," Feb 23, 1944.

44. ER, *If You Ask Me*, 18.

45. Ibid., 68.

46. ER, "Some of My Best Friends Are Negro," *Ebony*, Nov 1975, 77.

47. Ibid.

48. Ibid.

49. Ibid.

50. Lash, *Eleanor and Franklin*, 532.

51. Interview by Mike Wallace, Nov 23, 1957, www.hrc.utexas.edu/multi media/video/2008/wallace/roosevelt_eleanor.html.

52. ER, "My Day," Jul 29, 1943.

53. Ibid., Aug 7, 1943.

54. ER, "A Challenge to American Sportsmanship," *Collier's*, Oct 16, 1943, 71.

55. ER, "My Day," May 21, 1941.

56. ER, *India and the Awakening East*, 33.

57. ER, *The Autobiography of Eleanor Roosevelt*, 417.

58. ER, "From the Melting Pot—an American Race," *Liberty*, Jul 14, 1945, 89.

Chapter 12. On Humanity and Human Characteristics

1. ER and Hickok, 78.

2. ER, "In Defense of Curiosity," *Saturday Evening Post*, Aug 24, 1935, 66.

3. ER, "This Troubled World," in ER, *Courage in a Dangerous World*, 94.

4. ER, *My Days*, 21.

5. ER, "My Day," Jan 5, 1939.

6. Ibid., Jun 28, 1939.

7. ER, "The Moral Basis of Democracy," in ER, *Courage in a Dangerous World*, 53.

8. ER, "My Day," Jan 4, 1941. Similar quotes: Lash, *A World of Love*, 36; and ER, "My Day," Jul 5, 1943.

9. ER, "My Day," Aug 12, 1942.

10. Ibid., Dec 13, 1943.

11. Ibid., Aug 9, 1943.

12. Ibid., Nov 3, 1943.

13. Lash, *A World of Love*, 101.

14. ER, "My Day," May 30, 1944.

15. Ibid., Jun 13, 1944.

16. Lash, *A World of Love*, 132.

17. ER, "My Day," Aug 19, 1944.

18. Ibid., Apr 18, 1945.

19. Wotkyns, 124.

20. ER, *If You Ask Me*, 61–62.

21. Ibid., 120.

22. ER, *You Learn by Living*, xii

23. Ibid., 137.

24. Ibid., 136.

25. ER, *The Autobiography of Eleanor Roosevelt*, 408.

26. Ibid., 413.

27. ER, *Tomorrow Is Now*, 62.

28. Ibid., 71.

29. Ibid., 77.

30. Ibid., 138.

31. ER, "My Day," Aug 13, 1943.

32. Ibid., Jun 21, 1944.

33. Ibid., Aug 8, 1945.

34. Ibid., Dec 20, 1950.

35. Ibid., Aug 10, 1943.

36. ER, *If You Ask Me*, 121.

37. ER, "My Day," Feb 16, 1946.

38. ER, "Keepers of Democracy," *Virginia Quarterly Review*, Jan 1939, 2.

39. ER, *You Learn by Living*, 41.

40. ER, *Tomorrow Is Now*, 119.

41. ER, "In Defense of Curiosity," *Saturday Evening Post*, Aug 24, 1935, 64.

42. Ibid., 65.

43. Ibid., 66.

44. ER, *You Learn by Living*, 18.

45. ER, *Eleanor Roosevelt's Book of Common Sense Etiquette*, ix.

46. ER, "My Day," Aug 2, 1941.

47. ER, *You Learn by Living*, 6.

48. Robert Bendiner, "Eleanor Roosevelt at a Youthful 70," *NYT*, Oct 10, 1954.

49. ER, *You Learn by Living*, 28.

50. Ibid., 63.

51. ER, "My Day," Jun 19, 1936.

52. Ibid.

53. Lash, *Eleanor: The Years Alone*, 29.

54. ER, *This I Remember*, 57.

55. ER, *The White House Press Conferences*, 9.

56. ER, *You Learn by Living*, 114.

57. Ibid., 125.

58. ER, "My Day," Jul 26, 1944.

59. Ibid., Dec 9, 1941.

60. "Mrs. Roosevelt, America's Most Unusual Woman," *Cairns Post* (Cairns, Australia), Sep 4, 1943.

61. *Reader's Digest*, Sep 1940, 84.

62. "Job Hints Offered by Mrs. Roosevelt," *NYT*, Jun 28, 1940.

63. ER, "How to Take Criticism," *Ladies' Home Journal*, Nov 1944, 171.

64. ER, "Building Character," *Parent's Magazine*, Jun 1931, 17.

65. ER, *If You Ask Me*, 93.

66. ER, *You Learn by Living*, 25.

67. Ibid., 32.

68. Ibid., 40.

69. Ibid., 65.

70. ER, *The Autobiography of Eleanor Roosevelt*, xv.

71. Ibid., 410. Similar quote: ER, *You Learn by Living*, 64.

72. ER, *You Learn by Living*, 70.

73. ER, "My Day," Jun 15, 1946.

74. ER, *If You Ask Me*, 72.

75. ER, "My Day," Apr 28, 1959.

76. ER and A. Roosevelt, 156–57.

77. ER, "My Day," Jan 5, 1946.

78. Ibid., Jan 24, 1942.

79. ER, *You Learn by Living*, 65.

80. ER, *Tomorrow Is Now*, 6.

81. ER, *You Learn by Living*, 73.

Chapter 13. On Emotions

1. Cook, 1: 16.

2. For quotes about her feelings for particular individuals, please see chapter 14, "On Relationships," and chapter 17, "Eleanor Roosevelt on Others."

3. ER, "My Day," Feb 23, 1943.

4. Ibid., Jan 7, 1948.

5. ER, *This I Remember*, 233–34.

6. ER, "Keepers of Democracy," *Virginia Quarterly Review*, Jan 1939, 2.

7. ER, *Courage in a Dangerous World*, 262.

8. ER, *You Learn by Living*, 25.

9. Ibid., 29.

10. Ibid., 30.

11. Ibid., 32.

12. ER, *Tomorrow Is Now,* xvii.

13. Ibid., 81.

14. ER, *You Learn by Living*, 168.

15. ER, *The Autobiography of Eleanor Roosevelt*, 402.

16. ER, *This Is My Story*, 41.

17. ER and Hickok, 79.

18. Ibid., 147.

19. Ibid., 197–98.

20. ER, "This Troubled World," in ER, *Courage in a Dangerous World*, 45–46.

21. ER, "My Day," Apr 1, 1939.

22. Ibid., Oct 20, 1939.

23. Ibid.

24. Lash, *A World of Love*, 11.

25. Ibid., 20.

26. Ibid., 104.

27. Ibid., 116.

28. ER, "My Day," Feb 8, 1944.

29. Ibid., Feb 29, 1944.

30. Gurewitsch, *Kindred Souls*, 101.
31. ER, "My Day," Mar 29, 1958.
32. ER, *The Autobiography of Eleanor Roosevelt*, 414.
33. ER, *Eleanor Roosevelt's Book of Common Sense Etiquette*, 440.
34. ER, "My Day," Nov 22, 1943.
35. ER, *If You Ask Me*, 54.
36. ER, "My Day," Jul 28, 1936.
37. ER, *You Learn by Living*, 101.
38. ER, *The Autobiography of Eleanor Roosevelt*, 414.
39. Cook, 1: 208.
40. Ibid., 1: 264.
41. ER, *This Is My Story*, 309.
42. ER, "My Day," Jun 28, 1939.
43. ER, *The White House Press Conferences*, 126.
44. ER, "The Moral Basis of Democracy," in ER, *Courage in a Dangerous World*, 57.
45. ER, "My Day," Sep 11, 1941.
46. ER, *This I Remember*, 230.
47. ER, *You Learn by Living*, 82.
48. Ibid., 96.
49. ER, "My Day," Aug 16, 1941.

Chapter 14. On Relationships

1. See Rowley, *Franklin and Eleanor*, 160–63; and Gurewitsch, 79–80.
2. See ER and Hickok.
3. ER, *This Is My Story*, 309.
4. ER, *My Days*, 16.
5. ER, "My Day," Aug 3, 1945.
6. Ibid.
7. Ibid.
8. ER, *Eleanor Roosevelt's Book of Common Sense Etiquette*, 439.
9. ER, "How to Take Criticism," *Ladies' Home Journal*, Nov 1944, 155.
10. ER, *You Learn by Living*, 86–87.
11. Ibid., 72.
12. ER, *This Is My Story*, 361.

13. Ibid., 364.
14. ER, "My Day," Aug 3, 1945.
15. Ibid., Apr 23, 1962.
16. Wotkyns, 203.
17. Kearney, 125.
18. ER, "Ten Rules for Success in Marriage," *Pictorial Review*, Dec 1931, 4.
19. Ibid., 4, 36.
20. ER, "Should Wives Work?," *Good Housekeeping*, Dec 1937, 29.
21. Ibid., 212.
22. ER, "My Day," Mar 29, 1941.
23. Ibid., Feb 8, 1944.
24. ER, *This I Remember*, 349.
25. Lash, *A World of Love*, 104.
26. ER, *If You Ask Me*, 73.
27. Ibid., 85.
28. Ibid., 97.
29. Gurewitsch, 48
30. Ibid., 53.
31. ER, *Eleanor Roosevelt's Book of Common Sense Etiquette*, 263.
32. ER, "Ten Rules for Success in Marriage," *Pictorial Review*, Dec 1931, 4.
33. Ibid., 36.
34. ER, *If You Ask Me*, 108.
35. ER, *India and the Awakening East*, 68.
36. ER, "Building Character," *Parent's Magazine*, Jun 1931, 17.
37. Ibid.
38. ER, *It's Up to the Women*, 130.
39. ER, *This Is My Story*, 219.
40. ER, "My Day," Nov 11, 1938.
41. Ibid., Jul 7, 1942.
42. Ibid., May 15, 1945.
43. ER, *If You Ask Me*, 146.
44. ER, *You Learn by Living*, 38.
45. Ibid., 120
46. Ibid., 121.
47. ER, *The Autobiography of Eleanor Roosevelt*, 412.
48. ER, *You Learn by Living*, 87–88.
49. Ibid., 120.

Chapter 15. Miscellaneous

1. *Meet the Press*, NBC TV, Sep 16, 1956.
2. "People," *Time*, Jun 10, 1929.
3. "First Lady Flies with Miss Earhart," *NYT*, Apr 21, 1933.
4. ER, "My Day," Jul 17, 1944.
5. Ibid., Mar 2, 1936.
6. ER, *If You Ask Me*, 37.
7. ER and Truman, 174.
8. Lash, *Eleanor: The Years Alone*, 255.
9. ER, *You Learn by Living*, 70.
10. ER, *Tomorrow Is Now*, 18.
11. "Charity Not Enough Says Mrs. Roosevelt," *NYT*, Jan 13, 1932. Similar quote: ER, "My Day," Mar 1, 1941.
12. "Roosevelts Plan Busy Christmas," *NYT*, Dec 20, 1938.
13. ER, "My Day," Jul 23, 1941.
14. ER, *If You Ask Me*, 106.
15. ER, *This I Remember*, 13.
16. ER, "My Day," Oct 29, 1947.
17. ER, *You Learn by Living*, xii.
18. Ibid.
19. Ibid., 151
20. ER, "My Day," Mar 5, 1942.
21. Ibid., May 8, 1945.
22. "Smith for President Will Be Demanded by State Convention," *NYT*, Apr 15, 1924.
23. ER, "My Day," May 7, 1945. Similar quote: ER, *You Learn by Living*, 123.
24. ER, *Tomorrow Is Now*, 120.
25. ER, "My Day," Aug 26, 1942.
26. ER, "Social Gains and Defense," in ER, *Courage in a Dangerous World*, 133. Similar quotes: ER, "My Day," Sep 6, 1945; and ER, *You Learn by Living*, 71.
27. ER, "How to Take Criticism," *Ladies' Home Journal*, Nov 1944, 155.
28. ER, *Eleanor Roosevelt, John Kennedy, and the Election of 1960: A Project of The Eleanor Roosevelt Papers*, www.gwu.edu/~erpapers/mep/displaydoc.cfm?docid=jfko9#jfko9no1.
29. ER, *You Learn by Living*, 157.
30. ER, *This I Remember*, 261.

31. ER, *The Autobiography of Eleanor Roosevelt*, 390.

32. ER, "My Day," Oct 15, 1945.

33. ER, "If You Ask Me," *McCall's Magazine*, Sep 1953.

34. ER and Hickok, 192.

35. Robert Bendiner, "Eleanor Roosevelt at a Youthful 70," *NYT*, Oct 10, 1954.

36. ER, *Tomorrow Is Now*, 127.

37. ER, *You Learn by Living*, 32.

38. Ibid., 67.

39. Ibid., 187.

40. Beasley, 56.

41. "First Lady Wears a Five-Year-Old Dress to Show It Pays to Buy Good Material," *NYT*, Apr 5, 1945.

42. ER, *If You Ask Me*, 119–20.

43. ER, "My Day," Dec 3, 1954.

44. ER, *It Seems to Me*, 2. There is some controversy regarding this quote as the editor does not cite a source. Similar quote: ER, "My Day," July 28, 1943.

45. ER, "My Day," Nov 26, 1942.

46. ER, *The Autobiography of Eleanor Roosevelt*, 404.

47. Ibid., 409.

48. ER, *Tomorrow Is Now*, 134.

49. Ibid., 135.

50. ER, *The White House Press Conferences*, 18.

51. "First Lady Urges Help for Maimed," *NYT*, Sep 22, 1943.

52. ER, "My Day," Dec 4, 1944.

53. ER, *The Eleanor Roosevelt Papers*, 1: 102.

54. ER, "My Day," May 13, 1955.

55. "The Vibrant First Hostess of the Land," *NYT*, May 14, 1933.

56. ER, "In Defense of Curiosity," *Saturday Evening Post*, Aug 24, 1935, 8.

57. ER, "My Day," Feb 17, 1942.

58. Ibid., Feb 29, 1944.

59. ER, *Tomorrow Is Now*, 63. Similar quote: ER, "In Defense of Curiosity," *Saturday Evening Post*, Aug 24, 1935, 8.

60. ER, "The Negro and Social Change," *Opportunity*, Jan 1936, 23.

61. ER, *This Is My Story*, 259–60.

62. ER, "My Day," Oct 14, 1947.

63. Ibid., Dec 4, 1943.

64. Wotkyns, 123–24.
65. ER, "My Day," Sep 8, 1944.
66. Ibid., Apr 17, 1945.
67. ER and Truman, 246.
68. Interview by Mike Wallace, Nov 23, 1957, www.hrc.utexas.edu/multi media/video/2008/wallace/roosevelt_eleanor.html.
69. ER, *You Learn by Living*, 197
70. ER, "My Day," Nov 5, 1958.
71. Ibid.
72. Ibid., Dec 13, 1961.
73. Ibid., Apr 3, 1936.
74. Cook, 1: 250.
75. Ibid., 1: 250.
76. ER, "My Day," Feb 4, 1936.
77. Ibid., Jul 28, 1936.
78. "President's Wife Tells of Memoirs," *NYT*, Feb 25, 1937.
79. ER, "My Day," Jan 25, 1936.
80. Ibid., Feb 23, 1940.
81. ER, "Social Gains and Defense," *Common Sense*, Mar 1941, 71–72.
82. Lash, *Love, Eleanor*, 66.
83. ER, *The Autobiography of Eleanor Roosevelt*, 409.
84. ER, *You Learn by Living*, 111.
85. Ibid., 59.
86. ER, *The Autobiography of Eleanor Roosevelt*, xix.
87. Ibid., 409.
88. ER, *Tomorrow Is Now*, 80.
89. ER, "My Day," Apr 12, 1943.
90. ER, *You Learn by Living*, 124.
91. ER, "My Day," Mar 4, 1936.
92. ER and Truman, 265.
93. ER, *You Learn by Living*, xi.
94. Ibid., 165.
95. ER, "My Day," Jun 28, 1944.
96. Ibid., Apr 26, 1945.
97. Ibid.
98. "First Lady Befriends Grim Young Delegates," *Life*, Feb 26, 1940, 20.
99. ER, "My Day," Oct 25, 1945.
100. Ibid., Nov 14, 1944.

101. ER, *What I Hope to Leave Behind*, 174.

102. ER, *The Autobiography of Eleanor Roosevelt*, 435.

103. ER, "My Day," Feb 20, 1936.

104. Ibid., Jan 11, 1941.

105. Ibid., Mar 24, 1941.

106. ER, "Women in Politics," *Good Housekeeping*, Jan 1940, 150.

107. "Mrs. Roosevelt Asks Foreign-Born to Help This Nation Win the War," *NYT*, Feb 27, 1942.

108. ER, "My Day," Mar 4, 1944.

109. Ibid.

110. Ibid., Nov 29, 1944.

111. ER, *If You Ask Me*, 31.

112. ER, "My Day," May 29, 1941.

113. Ibid., Oct 30, 1943.

114. "Mrs. Roosevelt Reserved," *NYT*, Mar 16, 1947.

115. ER, "My Day," Jul 17, 1943.

116. ER, *My Days*, 24.

117. ER, "My Day," Oct 25, 1945.

118. ER, *The White House Press Conferences*, 160.

119. ER, "My Day," Feb 20, 1936.

120. Ibid., Jan 27, 1953.

121. ER, *You Learn by Living*, 153.

122. "Mrs. Roosevelt Wants 'Just a Little Job,'" *NYT*, Oct 8, 1944.

123. ER, *If You Ask Me*, 117.

124. ER, *You Learn by Living*, 118.

125. Ibid.

126. Ibid., 119.

127. ER, "My Day," Sep 22, 1941.

128. Ibid., Feb 5, 1943.

129. ER, *You Learn by Living*, 55.

130. Ibid.

131. Ibid., 60.

132. ER, *Tomorrow Is Now*, 38.

133. ER, "My Day," Mar 2, 1942.

134. Ibid., May 28, 1943.

135. "Mrs. Roosevelt Wants 'Just a Little Job,'" *NYT*, Oct 8, 1944.

136. ER, *Eleanor Roosevelt's Book of Common Sense Etiquette*, 206.

137. ER, *The White House Press Conferences*, 48.

138. ER, "My Day," Jun 9, 1943.

139. Ibid., Jul 14, 1943.

Chapter 16. On Herself

1. "National Affairs, Eleanor Roosevelt," *Time*, Nov 20, 1933.

2. ER, *This Is My Story*, 12.

3. ER, *You Learn by Living*, 3.

4. Roosevelt and Brough, *An Untold Story*, 25.

5. Helena Huntington Smith, "Profiles, Noblesse Oblige," *New Yorker*, Apr 5, 1930.

6. Beasley, 66. Similar quote: ER, *It's Up to the Women*, 260.

7. Hickok, 88.

8. ER and A. Roosevelt, 68.

9. ER and Hickok, 178.

10. Beasley, 110.

11. ER, *This Is My Story*, 171.

12. Lash, *Love, Eleanor*, 312.

13. ER, "My Day," Oct 23, 1940.

14. ER, "Insuring Democracy," *Collier's*, Jun 15, 1940, 70.

15. ER, *If You Ask Me*, 47.

16. Virginia Pasley, "Mrs. Roosevelt Lists Herself as 'Housewife,'" *Washington Times-Herald*, Mar 17, 1942.

17. ER, "My Day," Jul 8, 1942.

18. Gurewitsch, 144.

19. "Mrs. Roosevelt Wants 'Just a Little Job,'" *NYT*, Oct 8, 1944.

20. ER, "My Day," Apr 19, 1945. Similar quote: ER, "Why I Do Not Choose to Run," *Look*, Jul 9, 1946.

21. ER, "My Day," Sep 28, 1945.

22. ER, *The Eleanor Roosevelt Papers*, 1: 185.

23. ER and A. Roosevelt, 211.

24. S. J. Woolf, "The New Chapter in Mrs. Roosevelt's Life," *NYT Magazine*, Dec 15, 1946.

25. ER, *If You Ask Me*, 84.

26. ER, *This I Remember*, 166.

27. Ibid., 175.

28. Ibid., 336.

29. James MacGregor Burns and Janet Thompson Burns, "Mrs. Roosevelt a Remarkable 75," *NYT*, Oct 4, 1959.
30. ER, *The Autobiography of Eleanor Roosevelt*, xix.
31. Ibid., 410.
32. Ibid., 412.
33. Ibid., 416.
34. Ibid., 428.
35. J. Roosevelt, *My Parents*, 296.
36. Wotkyns, 133.
37. Lash, *Eleanor: The Years Alone*, 83.
38. ER, *You Learn by Living*, 32.
39. Cook, 1: 461.
40. Hickok, 2.
41. Beasley, 25. Similar quote: Hickok, 85.
42. Hickok, 118.
43. "Crowd Mind Read by Mrs. Roosevelt," *NYT*, Mar 5, 1933.
44. ER, "My Day," Jan 7, 1936.
45. Ibid.
46. ER and Hickok, 186.
47. Ibid., 195.
48. Ibid., 202.
49. ER, *This Is My Story*, 154.
50. ER and Hickok, 234.
51. Lash, *Eleanor and Franklin*, 792.
52. "1,000 Pay Homage to Mrs. Roosevelt," *NYT*, Jan 25, 1941.
53. Lash, *A World of Love*, 66.
54. ER, "Why I Do Not Choose to Run," *Look*, Jul 9, 1946.
55. Ibid.
56. ER, *If You Ask Me*, 54.
57. ER, *This I Remember*, 162.
58. Ibid., 350–51.
59. Lash, *Eleanor: The Years Alone*, 216, citing *New York Post*, Nov 18, 1952, letter to Bernard Baruch.
60. Gurewitsch, 3.
61. ER, *What I Hope to Leave Behind*, 282.
62. Lash, *Eleanor and Franklin*, 387.
63. ER, "Wives of Great Men," in ER, *What I Hope to Leave Behind*, 217.

64. ER, *This Is My Story*, 173.

65. ER, "My Day," Feb 23, 1942.

66. "'No' by Mrs. Roosevelt," *NYT*, Jun 13, 1947. Similar quotes: ER, "My Day," Apr 19, 1945; ER, *The Eleanor Roosevelt Papers*, 36; and interview by Mike Wallace, Nov 23, 1957, www.hrc.utexas.edu/multime dia/video/2008/wallace/roosevelt_eleanor.html.

67. ER, *This I Remember*, 8. Similar quote: Robert Bendiner, "Eleanor Roosevelt at a Youthful 70," *NYT*, Oct 10, 1954.

68. Robert Bendiner, "Eleanor Roosevelt at a Youthful 70," *NYT*, Oct 10, 1954.

69. ER, *You Learn by Living*, 72.

70. Cook, 1: 219.

71. ER, *The White House Press Conferences*, 201.

72. ER, "My Day," Aug 20, 1943.

73. Hickok, 28.

74. Rowley, 175. Similar quote: "As far as I am concerned, I cannot imagine living in fear of possible death," in "Mrs. Roosevelt Keeps to Routine," *NYT*, Feb 17, 1933.

75. "Mrs. Roosevelt Keeps to Routine," *NYT*, Feb 17, 1933. Similar quote: Hickok, 83.

76. Cook, 1: 491.

77. ER, "My Day," Jun 9, 1936.

78. Ibid., Oct 19, 1942.

79. "First Lady, in Oral Diary of White House, Reveals President's Refusal to 'Worry,'" *NYT*, Nov 17, 1936.

80. ER, *If You Ask Me*, 86.

Chapter 17. Eleanor Roosevelt on Others

1. Lash, *Eleanor and Franklin*, 245.

2. ER, *The Autobiography of Eleanor Roosevelt*, 47.

3. ER, *This Is My Story*, 1.

4. Ibid., 4. Similar quote: Elliott Roosevelt, *Hunting Big Game in the Eighties*, viii.

5. Cook, 1: 249.

6. Ibid., 1: 329.

7. "Mrs. Roosevelt Wants 'Just a Little Job,'" *NYT*, Oct 8, 1944.

8. ER, "My Day," Jan 13, 1941. Similar quote: ER, *This Is My Story*, 340.

9. Looker, *This Man Roosevelt*, 140.

10. ER, *The Autobiography of Eleanor Roosevelt*, 160.

11. Beasley, 96.

12. ER and Hickok, 210.

13. ER, "My Day," Oct 5, 1936.

14. ER and Hickok, 218.

15. Ibid., 270.

16. ER, "My Day," May 12, 1945.

17. ER, *This I Remember*, 67.

18. Ibid., 68.

19. Ibid., 73.

20. "4th-Term Decision News to First Lady," *NYT*, Jul 12, 1944.

21. ER, "My Day," Sep 4, 1941.

22. Ibid., Feb 21, 1936.

23. Ibid., Nov 9, 1945.

24. Ibid., May 19, 1941.

25. Ibid., Feb 19, 1943.

26. "Mrs. Roosevelt Hits Mme. Chiang: Says She Could Talk about Democracy but Didn't Know How to Live it," *Boston Post*, Dec 5, 1945.

27. ER, "My Day," Apr 29, 1941.

28. Interview by Mike Wallace, Nov 23, 1957, www.hrc.utexas.edu/multimedia/video/2008/wallace/roosevelt_eleanor.html.

29. ER, "My Day," May 25, 1942.

30. ER, *If You Ask Me*, 61.

31. Ibid.

32. ER, "My Day," Feb 11, 1944.

33. ER and Hickok, 72.

34. Lash, *Eleanor: The Years Alone*, 206.

35. ER and Hickok, 23.

36. Ibid., 183. Similar quote: "Mrs. Roosevelt Wants 'Just a Little Job,'" *NYT*, Oct 8, 1944.

37. ER and Hickok, 183.

38. ER, *The Autobiography of Eleanor Roosevelt*, 436.

39. ER, "My Day," Feb 1, 1960.

40. Hareven, *Eleanor Roosevelt*, 260.

41. ER, "My Day," Apr 19, 1945.

42. ER, *The Eleanor Roosevelt Papers*, 48.

Chapter 18. Others on Eleanor Roosevelt

1. Gurewitsch, 148.
2. Beasley, 170.
3. "A First First Lady," *Democratic Digest*, Mar 1, 1935, 7.
4. Gurewitsch, 171.
5. "Women: First Lady," *Time*, Oct 25, 1948.
6. Longworth and Teague, *Mrs. L.*, 155.
7. Interview by Mike Wallace, Nov 23, 1957, www.hrc.utexas.edu/multi media/video/2008/wallace/roosevelt_eleanor.html.
8. "Eulogy Stirs Cheers for Mrs. Roosevelt," *NYT*, Jun 25, 1936.
9. Rowley, 21.
10. Smith, 181.
11. Catt, et al., 178.
12. Wotkyns, 91.
13. Lash, *A World of Love*, vii.
14. J. Roosevelt, 25.
15. "The Hour and the Men," *Saturday Review of Literature*, Jan 6, 1951, 11.
16. Rowley, 22, citing a Feb 18, 1901, letter to Mary Hall, FDR Library.
17. "NAACP Tributes to Mrs. Eleanor Roosevelt," *Crisis*, Dec 1962.
18. "President Kennedy Leads Nation in Expressing Sorrow at Death of Mrs. Roosevelt," *NYT*, Nov 8, 1962.
19. "Women: First Lady," *Time*, Oct 25, 1948.
20. Gurewitsch, 291.
21. Harrity and Martin, *Eleanor Roosevelt*, 207–8.

Bibliography

Asbell, Bernard. *When F.D.R. Died*. New York: Holt, Rinehart and Winston, 1961.

Bassett, Margaret Byrd. *Profiles and Portraits of American Presidents and Their Wives*. Freeport, Me.: B. Wheelwright, 1964.

Beasley, Maurine H. *Eleanor Roosevelt and the Media: A Public Quest for Self-Fulfillment*. Urbana: University of Illinois Press, 1987.

Beasley, Maurine H., Holly C. Shulman, and Henry R. Beasley, eds. *The Eleanor Roosevelt Encyclopedia*. Westport, Conn.: Greenwood Press, 2001.

Black, Allida M. *Casting Her Own Shadow: Eleanor Roosevelt and the Shaping of Postwar Liberalism*. New York: Columbia University Press, 1996.

Black, Ruby A. *Eleanor Roosevelt: A Biography*. New York: Duell, Sloan and Pearce, 1940.

Brands, H. W. *Traitor to His Class: The Privileged Life and Radical Presidency of Franklin Delano Roosevelt*. New York: Doubleday, 2008.

Catt, Carrie Chapman, Eleanor Roosevelt, and National Committee on the Cause and Cure of War. *Why Wars Must Cease*. Edited by Rose Young. New York: Macmillan, 1935.

Cook, Blanche Wiesen. *Eleanor Roosevelt*. Vol. 1, *1884–1933*; Vol. 2, *1934–1962*. New York: Viking, 1992, 1999.

Davis, Kenneth S. *Invincible Summer: An Intimate Portrait of the Roosevelts Based on the Recollections of Marion Dickerman*. New York: Atheneum, 1974.

Faber, Doris. *The Life of Lorena Hickok: E.R.'s Friend*. New York: Morrow, 1960.

Farr, Finis. *The Life of Westbrook Pegler*. New Rochelle, N.Y.: Arlington House, 1975.

Francis, Charles E. *The Tuskegee Airmen: The Men Who Changed a Nation*. New Rochelle, N.Y.: Arlington House, 1975.

Glendon, Mary Ann. *A World Made New: Eleanor Roosevelt and the Universal Declaration of Human Rights*. New York: Random House, 2001.

Goodwin, Doris Kearns. *No Ordinary Time: Franklin and Eleanor Roosevelt: The Home Front in World War II*. New York: Simon and Schuster, 1994.

Gurewitsch, Edna P. *Kindred Souls: The Friendship of Eleanor Roosevelt and David Gurewitsch*. New York: St. Martin's Press, 2002.

Hareven, Tamara K. *Eleanor Roosevelt: An American Conscience*. Chicago: Quadrangle, 1968.

Harrity, Richard, and Ralph G. Martin. *Eleanor Roosevelt: Her Life in Pictures*. New York: Duell, Sloan and Pearce, 1958.

Hickok, Lorena. *Reluctant First Lady*. New York: Dodd, Mead, 1962.

Kearney, James R. *Anna Eleanor Roosevelt: The Evolution of a Reformer*. Boston: Houghton Mifflin, 1968.

Lash, Joseph P. *Eleanor: The Years Alone*. New York: Norton, 1972.

———. *Eleanor and Franklin*. New York: Norton, 1971.

———. *Life Was Meant to Be Lived: A Centenary Portrait of Eleanor Roosevelt*. New York: Norton, 1984.

———. *Love, Eleanor: Eleanor Roosevelt and Her Friends*. New York: Doubleday, 1982.

———. *A World of Love: Eleanor Roosevelt and Her Friends, 1943–1962*. Garden City, N.Y.: Doubleday, 1984.

Longworth, Alice Roosevelt, and Michael Teague. *Mrs. L.: Conversations with Alice Roosevelt Longworth*. Garden City, N.Y.: Doubleday, 1981.

Looker, Earle. *This Man Roosevelt*. New York: Brewer, Warren and Putnam, 1932.

Mackenzie, Compton. *Mr. Roosevelt*. New York: Dutton, 1944.

Morsink, Johannes. *The Universal Declaration of Human Rights: Origins, Drafting and Intent*. Philadelphia: University of Pennsylvania Press, 1999.

Pederson, William D. *The FDR Years*. New York: Facts on File, 2006.

Roosevelt, Eleanor. *The Autobiography of Eleanor Roosevelt*. New York: Harper and Brothers, 1961.

———. *Courage in a Dangerous World: The Political Writings of Eleanor Roosevelt*. Edited by Allida M. Black. New York: Columbia University Press, 1999.

———. *Eleanor Roosevelt's Book of Common Sense Etiquette*. New York: Macmillan, 1962.

———. *If You Ask Me*. New York: D. Appleton Century, 1946.

———. *India and the Awakening East*. New York: Harper and Brothers, 1953.

———. *It Seems to Me: Selected Letters of Eleanor Roosevelt*. Edited by Leonard C. Schlup and Donald W. Whisenhunt. Lexington: University Press of Kentucky, 2001.

———. *It's Up to the Women*. New York: Frederick A. Stokes, 1933.

———. *My Days*. New York: Dodge, 1938.

———. *On My Own*. New York: Harper and Brothers, 1958.

———. *The Eleanor Roosevelt Papers*. Vol. 1, *The Human Rights Years, 1945–1948*. Edited by Allida M. Black. Detroit: Gale, 2007.

———. *The White House Press Conferences of Eleanor Roosevelt*. Edited by Maurine Beasley. New York: Garland, 1983.

———. *This I Remember*. New York: Harper and Brothers, 1949.

———. *This Is My Story*. New York: Garden City Publishing, 1937.

———. *Tomorrow Is Now*. New York: Harper and Row, 1963.

———. *You Learn by Living*. New York: Harper, 1960.

———. *What I Hope to Leave Behind: The Essential Essays of Eleanor Roosevelt*. Edited by Allida M. Black. New York: Carlson, 1995.

Roosevelt, Eleanor, and Lorena A. Hickok. *Empty without You: The Intimate Letters of Eleanor Roosevelt and Lorena Hickok*. Edited by Rodger Streitmatter. New York: Free Press, 1998.

Roosevelt, Eleanor, and Anna Roosevelt. *Mother & Daughter: The Letters of Eleanor and Anna Roosevelt*. Edited by Bernard Asbell. New York: Coward, McCann and Geoghegan, 1982.

Roosevelt, Eleanor, and Harry S. Truman. *Eleanor and Harry: The Correspondence of Eleanor Roosevelt and Harry S. Truman*. Edited by Steve Neal. New York: Scribner, 2002.

Roosevelt, Elliott. *Hunting Big Game in the Eighties: The Letters of Elliott Roosevelt, Sportsman*. Edited by Anna Eleanor Roosevelt [ER]. New York: Scribner, 1933.

Roosevelt, Elliott, and James Brough. *An Untold Story: The Roosevelts of Hyde Park*. New York: Putnam Sons, 1973.

———. *Mother R: Eleanor Roosevelt's Untold Story*. New York: Putnam Sons, 1977.

Roosevelt, James. *My Parents: A Differing View*. Chicago: Playboy Press, 1976.

Rowley, Hazel. *Franklin and Eleanor: An Extraordinary Marriage*. New York: Farrar, Straus and Giroux, 2010.

Smith, Jean Edward. *FDR*. New York: Random House, 2007.

The Academy: A Weekly Review of Literature & Life. London: Clement's Printing Works, 1901.

The Eleanor Roosevelt Papers Project. "My Day Project." www.gwu.edu /~erpapers/myday/.

———. Online Documents and videos. www.gwu.edu/%7Eerpapers/doc uments/.

———. Travel around the World. www.gwu.edu/~erpapers/maps/1952_ trip.html.

Wotkyns, Eleanor R. *With Love, Aunt Eleanor: Stories from My Life with the First Lady of the World*. Petaluma, Calif.: Scrapbook Press, 2004.

Michele Wehrwein Albion, a former museum curator, is the author of *The Florida Life of Thomas Edison* and the editor of *The Quotable Edison* and *The Quotable Henry Ford*. She lives in New Hampshire with her husband and four children.

The University Press of Florida is the scholarly publishing agency for the State University System of Florida, comprising Florida A&M University, Florida Atlantic University, Florida Gulf Coast University, Florida International University, Florida State University, New College of Florida, University of Central Florida, University of Florida, University of North Florida, University of South Florida, and University of West Florida.